We're Not All EGOMANIACS

Adapting the Twelve Steps for Alcoholics with Low Self-Esteem

Beth Aich

Edited by Heidi Mitchell

General Disclaimer

DEDICATION

This book is dedicated to the unknown number of alcoholics with low self-esteem who either left Alcoholics Anonymous or stayed even though it was painful and psychologically damaging, because there was nowhere else to go. You are not alone, and I hope you will give it another try.

CONTENTS

Acknowledgments 1

Introduction 3

1. My Story 9

2. Some Definitions 35

3. A Brief History of the AA Program 42

4. Egomaniacs and Shame-Based People 47

5. What Does Childhood Have to Do With Low Self-Esteem? 55

6. Feelings 69

7. Step Zero 80

8. Step One 91

9. Step Two 96

10. Step Three 99

11. Step Four 103

12. Step Five 113

13. Step Six 114

14. Step Seven 116

15. Step Eight 118

16. Step Nine 121

17. Step Ten 124

18. Step Eleven 129

19. Step Twelve 133

Endnotes 135

Bibliography 139

Table 1. Comparison of Egomaniac and Shame-based Tendencies 51

Table 2. Affirmations 83

Table 3. Self vs. Friend 86

ACKNOWLEDGMENTS

Thanks to Pia Mellody for seeing me through the first three years of my journey, to my friend Jay for the saying about funhouse mirrors and gaslights, to my therapist Dr. Susan for all the family of origin work and encouragement in writing the book, to my sponsor Becky for always being supportive, to my sister Katie for validating my childhood memories, to the Secular AA community for permitting open discussion rather than only endorsement of the AA program, and to the many, many AA members who have been a part of my recovery.

INTRODUCTION

I am writing this book because I believe there are many people like me who come into AA with an ego that has been crushed, rather than one that needs to be deflated. In early sobriety, I kept trying to see myself as the personality type described in the first 164 pages of the *Big Book of Alcoholics Anonymous*[1] because people were accepting it as gospel and told me I needed to, too, if I wanted to stay sober. Having a weakly defined sense of self, full of self-doubt, and constantly second-guessing my thoughts and feelings, I was vulnerable to allowing others to define me. I started telling myself I was selfish and self-centered because that's what the book said. I told myself my ego was too big, that I was constantly running around stepping on others' toes and trying to control things, knowing that I could be happy if everyone only did what I wanted them to do. Telling myself these things made my self-esteem even worse. In my mind, the worst things a person can do are be selfish and step on toes. After many years in recovery, I realized I have never been an egomaniac, never thought I was God, usually feel undeserving rather than entitled, don't think I know best, don't try to control others, and am far more concerned about the happiness of others than my own. I came in at the opposite end of the spectrum from Bill W. My ego needed building, not deflating. AA can absolutely work for people like me, and it has, but some parts of the program need a little tweaking.

I'm extremely grateful to AA for my sobriety. One alcoholic talking to another is pure magic. It allows us to drop the fear of being judged and become honest and authentic, at least with other alcoholics. That's a start. Meetings provide a safe place to share, which is huge for those of us who have never learned how, or been taught not to, talk about what's going on inside us. Without this secure, loving environment, we would never take those risks. By listening, we learn we are not the only person on the planet who feels the way we do, and we learn about other ways of handling things. We all admit we're works in progress, not perfect. My group told me, "We'll love you until you learn to love yourself"—and they did.

I learned what unconditional love means in AA, which was something I had never experienced. It means no matter who you are or what you've done, you are welcome. People who may not agree on anything else still have each other's backs when it comes to staying sober. The love shown to someone back from a relapse is something to behold—love that is not tied to performance, almost the opposite. These people are usually heaping plenty of shame and judgment on themselves. We extend even more love to them because they are hurting.

Introducing myself is a shame reduction technique. I say, "I'm Beth, I'm an alcoholic," and everyone responds with "Hi, Beth," instead of "Shame on you. You're a disgrace." I learned how to look at my issues in an analytical format (Step Four) that helps me figure out what's really going on with me. Not keeping secrets, making amends, and continuing to work on the areas that need improving has become a way of life. And working with others is still one of the great joys of my life today.

This book is not intended to denigrate in any way the positive impact that AA has had on the lives of so many people, including me, nor to disparage the founders and their great accomplishment. The early AA members all seem to have had the egomaniac type personality, and they developed a program that worked for them. They just weren't clairvoyant about additional types of personalities that would later be joining AA, and they can't be faulted for that. Nor is this book intended to replace *Alcoholics Anonymous* (hereinafter the *Big Book*) or *Twelve*

Steps and Twelve Traditions[2] (hereinafter the *Twelve & Twelve*), and in fact, it assumes you are using them. This book is an adjunct. It does not deal with topics thoroughly covered in AA literature. It is meant to fill in the spaces where the low self-esteem personality type was left out.

I am not suggesting these are the only two personality types in AA or even that personality is the dominant factor in everyone's alcoholism. Other people's experiences may be way different from mine, and hopefully, they will write their own books. The more models of what recovery can look like for different people, the better. *No one can be pigeonholed into authenticity.*

I have synthesized ideas and concepts from many different fields. I am not an expert in any of them, and I reference many other sources for you to check out. My only expertise is in what worked for me. My hope is that you will be able to make a program that works for you.

I strongly encourage anyone struggling with childhood trauma and/or mental illness to seek outside help as I did. These issues absolutely affect our ability to stay sober, but they are beyond the scope of AA and this book.

The book begins with telling my story. I want to give you an idea of the factors that shaped me into a person who drank to live and lived to drink and what needed to change after I got sober. I realize my exact circumstances are unique to me. There are many ways to end up with low self-esteem. I hope you can identify with the feelings or, as they say, look for the similarities, not the differences. My story is quite long, but please bear with me; I wanted to give you lots of examples.

From there, we look at who the early AA members were and their reason for designing twelve steps to deflate the ego. I've listed some character traits of egomaniacs and of people with low self-esteem, so you can see the issues that people like me have, compared to people for whom the program was written. If you are like me, your ego needs to be built up, not deflated. But that doesn't mean we throw the program out! The Steps are a tool for self-discovery, and they work for us, too. AA meetings and the fellowship provide a nurturing environment where it is safe to discover our true selves without being silenced or judged. We need that.

In the next few chapters, we look at some causes of low self-esteem, which is usually acquired during childhood, and how to manage our feelings so that we have other options besides picking up a drink to make them go away. We wouldn't be here if that strategy worked.

The remainder of the book goes through each of the Twelve Steps, acknowledging that some of the language and exercises outlined in AA literature are triggers for us to feel even more ashamed of ourselves. Now we know we are not alone in having those feelings and can remind ourselves that these words were written for a different audience. Yes, we're all alcoholics, but not all alcoholics are the same. I hope to spare you some of the pain I went through, being a willing and compliant newcomer, and ending up feeling even worse about myself. But the main focus is on tweaking the Steps to be tools for building self-esteem. Most chapters have additional exercises for the step, or the step has been reframed in a positive rather than punitive way.

Step Twelve is the grand finale. Having attained enough self-esteem to know and love ourselves, we can be uniquely useful to newcomers who feel like we did when we came in. What a joy that is!

A Word about Traditional AA

When people attempt to change anything about the program or the Twelve Steps, or even comment on the *Big Book* in any way that is short of a full endorsement, it can be met with not only resistance but outright hostility. I understand that AA has worked for millions of people exactly the way it was written. I have no quarrel whatsoever with that and do not expect those people to read this book. They have found what works for them, and I'm happy for them.

In his own later writings, however, Bill did not take this dogmatic stance about the program. In his *Grapevine* articles, he reflected on the success of AA. In the April 1961 edition, he noted that although AA had saved many people over the past twenty-five years, there were even more who came in but left. This is a far cry from, "Rarely have we seen a person fail who has thoroughly followed our path."[3] He acknowledged that some of these failures were not the fault of the newcomers, but that AA had likely failed them in some way. He confessed that he nearly ruined AA in the early years with the demand that everyone must get the God of *his* understanding. He admitted to having an "unconscious arrogance" about his way being right for everyone, which is typical of egomaniacs. He couldn't see it in himself at four years of sobriety, but he did later. Maybe some people left because they felt like the worst person that ever lived and were told they had too *much* ego and lacked humility.

As far as the sanctity of the Steps goes, it may surprise you to learn that not a single one of the first hundred sober men who were around when Bill wrote the *Big Book* had worked them as written.[4] That's because they didn't exist in that form until he wrote the book. "Here are the steps we took…" is not true. None of the stories in the first edition of the *Big Book* mention working the Twelve Steps.

In *AA Comes of Age*, Bill talked about the spread of AA into other countries, including Thailand, a largely Buddhist country.[5] Buddha was a man, not a god. After reading the Steps, a Buddhist priest said he would change the word "God" to "good" and then they could go along with it. Bill was totally fine with that. He said the Steps were only suggestions; AA did not require a belief in them as written; and this was good because it opened the door to more suffering alcoholics.

The Bill W. of later years likely would not have objected to the ideas in this book. Since we continue to grow in the program, most everyone with long-term sobriety feels they know more now than they did when they had only four years. Bill was no exception, and he did write about his changed views, but he never went back and changed the book.

My point is for you to understand that you are not doomed to drink because you changed the magic formula, even though some people may tell you that.

1

MY STORY

What It Was Like

My sobriety date is September 29, 1985. That's the break between my before and after story. You can't change the past, but you can certainly change the way you see it.

I was raised in a socioeconomically privileged family. We had nice things and took fun trips. We had a boat and enjoyed family outings. We belonged to a country club, and my siblings and I swam on the swim team. We went to church, sang in the choir, got good grades, and were good kids. On the outside, we looked pretty normal, even fortunate. I have many fond memories of time spent with siblings. We had a lot of fun together. Eventually, there were six of us, four girls and two boys. I will not be talking about them much out of respect for their privacy. I do mention one sister quite often, but it's not her real name. I will say this: among us as a group, there have been serious alcohol and drug problems, anorexia and bulimia, depression, and suicide attempts—all coming from this normal-looking family.

I'm going to include in my story childhood memories that have stuck with me to this day because they shaped me into a person who needed alcohol to cope with life. The incidents I will describe really didn't seem like a big deal to me at the time. It was life as usual. That's because I didn't know any better or have anything to compare it with until later. In fact, AA is the first place where I ever saw people make a distinction between a person and their behavior: "We love you, we all make mistakes, and we've got your back; you will be supported no matter what you are going through." Come to find out, parents are supposed to be like that, too.

I remember being yelled at and told, "Shame on you! You're a disgrace! There's no excuse for you!" many times when I didn't even know I had done something wrong. Or, in retrospect, the condemnation was at best extremely disproportionate to what I had done wrong. We were routinely called onto the carpet and scolded so harshly I wished I could just disappear into the floor rather than stand there feeling so naked and exposed. There was no distinction between having done something wrong and being a bad person. When I talk later about having a shame attack, it means I am reliving this feeling. When this happens, I am immobilized and can't hear or process anything.

I never thought my parents were wrong; I thought I really must be that bad. So, these aren't bad childhood memories of when I was aware of being abused; to me, they were normal things that happened to bad kids who deserved it.

There were countless occasions when I wanted or needed something from my mother and she would give me this warning look that said, *Don't make me put my book down.* Then she would answer me:

- "Can't you make do just once?"
- "You are not sick (or hurt or hungry); you just think you are."
- "You were born with a silver spoon in your mouth; how dare you ask for more!"
- "Stop being so selfish."

- "There's nothing wrong with you. You're just trying to get attention."

Frequently, she would just glare with a look of disgust, contempt, or hate and not answer at all.

I learned I was a burden and not worth taking care of. Sometimes she was in a nurturing mood and would help; I just never knew which way it would be. My siblings and I frequently "walked on eggshells" till we knew what kind of mood Mom was in. I learned to not trust my perceptions of reality. I feel hungry but she says I can't be. I feel sick but she says I'm just trying to get sympathy. I'm upset but she says I'm not; I just want attention.

In grade school, I frequently had the same teacher my sister had had the year before. My dad fostered competition among the siblings, and I always felt the need to promote myself over my much cuter sister. (It was an accepted fact in the family that Katie was the cute one. I was labeled the smart one.) I told the kindergarten teacher that Katie said she was a dumbbell, which was true. Somehow my parents were notified, and they made me write an apology letter that said I was a dumbbell for saying that. I was too ashamed to deliver it and "accidentally" dropped it on the way to school. I didn't understand why I was in trouble because I had told the truth; Katie was the one who had said it. The irony was that even in kindergarten I was perfectly capable of writing a note that said I am a dumbbell. It's doubly shaming when you're not only bad but too stupid to understand why.

One time when I was about four, Mom walked a bunch of neighborhood kids to the store for candy, but she made me get cottage cheese because I was a little on the chubby side. Some older kids were coming in as we were leaving, and they all pointed and made fun of me. I felt ashamed and ostracized. When I was five or six, my mother returned from Christmas shopping, and I observed her taking a doll out of the car. I saw a terrible wrong about to happen and quickly informed her that she wasn't supposed to buy that because one of my sisters asked Santa Claus to bring it. She glared at me with utter contempt and said, "Do you really think reindeer can fly?" Boy, did I feel stupid and ashamed, not to mention I just lost Santa Claus.

When Mom lost her temper, she hit us with a shoe or a hairbrush or anything she could reach. Dad used a paddle which hung on the kitchen wall. We also had our mouths washed out with soap. I never thought of this as abuse; it happened to some of our friends, too.

When I was seven, I came upon my baby brother in an upstairs bathroom drinking Drano. Mom was downstairs reading, and no one was watching him. He had his stomach pumped three times as a toddler. We were not well supervised. We also didn't wash our hands before eating or after going to the bathroom. I only started doing that when I noticed other people doing it. We ate food that was left out on top of the stove for three days. But we knew how to set a table with every little thing in the right place, and which fork to use when, because we were Episcopalians.

When I was eight or nine and had been sent to my room "in disgrace" again, I tried to turn the tables on my mother and asked her, "If I am so awful, then why did you have me?" She didn't respond, but it didn't matter because I already knew the answer. They didn't know I was going to be this awful before I was born; I did it all myself. I was an utter disappointment. Today I notice that after kids are sent to their rooms, a parent usually goes and talks to them about what happened and then they come out together. That didn't happen in my house. At some point, we were allowed to come out, but the critical part was missing—first a discussion of the behavior, a talk about feelings, what have we learned, and then being reunited, welcomed back into the fold.

I was well behaved in grade school, but one day we had a substitute teacher and I was talking when I wasn't supposed to be. She pointed at me and said, "You, in the green dress!" I not only felt ashamed at that moment but all over again every time I saw that dress in my closet. I never wore it again. I realize today that was an oversized reaction. It had triggered me to relive other shame episodes.

When Katie was in third grade, my mom's father took her on a trip and molested her. It was talked about when they got back, but they didn't do anything because it would be too embarrassing; he was the attorney for my father's business. Two years later, they let him take me on a trip. Today I find that astounding, outrageous even, that they didn't protect me because it might cause uncomfortable feelings in the family. He did not molest me, and I assumed I was being rejected as too ugly. He went on to molest several other children before he died. My parents also allowed my mother's alcoholic mother to drive us around when she was drunk because that was easier than confronting the problem.

I was fat-shamed by both parents. I had learned not to go to my mom for comfort and Dad was never home, so my comfort came from candy. Every month or so, my father would take all us kids to the store and let us buy all the junk food we wanted. We called it "glop-shopping." Then we'd all come home and pig out. He also bought doughnuts on Saturday mornings—maybe six dozen for seven people. No one was teaching healthy eating. My dad also had a special nickname for me when I was little. He called me "Flapjaw" because I talked too much. It was weird, feeling kind of special because I got a nickname but an unflattering one.

Starting in junior high, in every new classroom, I would do a quick scan to see if I was the fattest girl because I hated being blindsided. If I was going to be teased, I wanted to know in advance. My greatest fear was, and still is to some extent, for someone to trigger my shame reaction without me seeing it coming. Because then I feel not only ashamed but stupid, too.

The summer I was fourteen, our eighteen-year-old swim team coach asked me out on a date. I was so flattered! Of course, I went along with it; beggars can't be choosers, you know. I had no idea what he saw in me. At the end of the summer, he went off to college and I started high school. The age difference was too great—he was writing me about drinking beer and growing a mustache, things I couldn't relate to at the time, so I didn't write back. In the middle of the night one night, my mother came into my bedroom, turned on the light like the Spanish Inquisition, and started scolding me. If I didn't write him back, he was going to be upset, it might affect his grades, he could lose his scholarship and have to drop out of college, and it would be all my fault! How could I be so thoughtless? (Apparently at fourteen, I had the power to ruin someone's life by not returning a letter.)

The manners we were taught were all about putting other people ahead of ourselves. Don't ever take the nicest or the best or the biggest whatever—it should go to someone else, never you. Don't take credit for anything. Never toot your own horn. Accept responsibility for everything bad that is remotely related to you. Always put others' needs ahead of your own. Nobody cares how you feel or what you think; it's more important to put on a good act. If you're inviting people to something, make sure that anyone who's not invited doesn't hear about it or their feelings will be hurt (no one can handle that, and it will be your fault). Rather than a sense of entitlement, I felt like I didn't deserve anything good. In seventh grade, I lost a student election by one vote. I had voted for the other person because I was being polite.

When I was around fifteen, I came home one time from being out with a group of friends and we must have had a fight, I don't even remember. We were probably friends again the next day. I walked into the house and said my friends were all stupid and I didn't need any friends anyway. Looking back, the no-brainer parental response would be, "What's wrong?" "What happened?" But my mother said, "If that's the way you feel, then I hate you." I ran up to my room crying. When I eventually came down, she said, "I'm glad you came down," and that's all that was ever said about it.

Around the age of sixteen, I was a little overweight and felt very unattractive because I was always in my cute sister's shadow. My father looked me up and down one day, like he did all women, comparing them to the perfect model in his mind, and burst out laughing. That was bad enough. Then, drawing on his family's background in the pork business, he told me I would make a good brood sow. I ran out of the room crying and for the longest time (decades) believed that when men look at me, they see a pig. Another time, seeking a little redemption, I asked him if I at least had good legs because they were very muscular. I happened to be standing in front of the baby grand, and he said, "Yes, for a piano." He also used to tell me I'd be pretty tall if so much of me wasn't turned under. After that, bowling became a major shaming experience for me because the shoe size is written on the outside, right where everyone can see it. Dad's benchmark for saying things seemed to be that it didn't matter how cruel it was if it was funny. You were supposed to laugh at the joke and "not be so sensitive." This is another example of gaslighting: I'm not cruel, you're too sensitive.

With Dad, I always had the sense of scarcity—not of material things but of love, appreciation, attention. The kids had to compete for his attention by outdoing each other. He valued achievements, not kindness or thoughtfulness, and the achievements had to be things he cared about, not what we were interested in. Years later, I realized I took this dynamic into the workplace whenever I had a male boss, always perceiving my coworkers as competitors. I couldn't be a worker among workers, because I experienced anyone else's gain as my loss. Even today, I still have a gut shame response when someone does something good—I should be doing that; I'm bad. For example, if someone says they worked out this morning, and I didn't—instantaneous shame reaction. One time after I was many years sober and a practicing attorney, Dad was reflecting on how he had been high school valedictorian, as had my son. Then he shook his head bewilderedly and said to me and my two sisters who were present, "I guess sometimes success just skips a generation." I had enough recovery at that point to laugh and say, "Or maybe they just don't define it the same way you do."

Dad valued performance so much that it was hard to try anything new. It was unacceptable to be bad at something. He didn't really allow for a learning curve. That held me back a lot. It was terrible going through my first pregnancy without alcohol (but no program) and having everyone see me do it. I knew I was probably doing it wrong. I could never comprehend how anyone could play baseball, knowing there's a good chance everyone is going to watch you strike out.

In high school, Mom bought us alcohol, used drugs with us, and bought the latest music; all our friends hung out at our house. We didn't know if they were coming to see her or us. She must have been reliving the teenage years she missed in her alcoholic home. One time, she picked up a twenty-year-old hippie hitchhiker and brought him home to sleep in the basement. She went out and left him with her seventeen, sixteen, and thirteen-year-old daughters. He turned us all onto acid. At the time, everyone was saying how cool our mother was, and I believed them. I was supposed to feel lucky for having such a cool mom.

In reality, I didn't have a mom at all. She didn't look out for our safety. She wasn't even a friend. Whenever a conflict arose, she always took the other person's side, never her own kid's. My father didn't approve of drugs, alcohol, and hippies hanging out, but he just stayed away and never confronted her. Fortunately for me (I thought at the time), Katie didn't really enjoy being in an altered state of consciousness. I began to hang out with hippies and drug users, so no more competition. I could make fun of her for being straight. (In all fairness to my sister, she never treated me like I was less than, and we are very close today. It was Dad and society doing that.)

I developed a defense mechanism I now call the "I reject you first" game: I don't want to belong to the group of boring, popular girls who don't drink or drug—they are so uncool. I don't want to be a cheerleader—there's a war going on and all they care about is high school football. I'm so much deeper than that. I'm on an airplane in my T-shirt and patched jeans looking at a thin, attractive, perfectly groomed flight attendant, and I think she's allowing herself to be exploited. I'm better than that. It was better to think that than face the reality that I wasn't good enough to be exploited.

I lost my faith at the age of sixteen. It was no big dispute with the church or anything. It was more like a cognitive awakening of the educational variety. I realized that if I had been born in Saudi Arabia, I would be a Muslim; in India, probably a Hindu; in Tibet, a Buddhist. It had nothing to do with truth but only what people were taught. I have nothing bad to say about the church I was raised in or the people who went there; it was lovely. I just stopped believing, the same way I would have stopped believing in Santa Claus given the chance. I'm not out to change anyone else's beliefs; this is just part of my story.

During the summers in high school, all our friends got jobs at a nearby amusement park. We wanted to, too, but Mom said no, we would be taking a job away from someone who couldn't go to college without it, whereas we still could (it was our responsibility to hold ourselves back and allow others to go ahead). The next summer we didn't ask, and she said, "You kids are so lazy. Why don't you get jobs?"

Around that time in history, there were a lot of slogans going around in pop culture, and I latched onto probably the worst one for someone like me: "If you're not part of the solution, you're part of the problem." That took me to new heights of responsibility, all the way down to reading labels on cans to see what country they came from because if I buy it, I'm condoning their human rights record. Paralyzed at the grocery store.

Looking back, I see that a few boys liked me in high school, but I couldn't relate to that. I thought something must be wrong with them.

I managed to get myself into an Ivy League college, but I took no credit for it. I thought they just accepted me because my grandfather had gone there. I was using drugs and alcohol just like I had at home, although my mother had stopped once the entourage was gone and there was no one to hold court with. I had a few blackout drunks. Freshman year, I had a boyfriend—my first adult sexual relationship. He was a junior, and he chose me! Again, I went along with it because I couldn't believe my good fortune. I was mostly living in his room, and one day I went down to my room to get some books. He was in bed with my roommate, listening to my stereo! The world as I knew it came crumbling down. I would forever be suspicious of anything that seemed too good to be true. I called my mom crying, and she said, "Why don't you come home for the weekend?" I did, but she wasn't around, never made herself available, and I went back thinking, What was the point of that?

She had come to my aid earlier that year when I broke my leg. I'll give her credit for that. She understood that a broken leg was a real injury. She did not understand emotional injury. I compounded the ankle injury by trying to walk on it because I imagined that if I lay on the ground and called for help, someone would say, "Hey! We've got a beached whale over here!"

That summer, we went on a trip to East Africa. I was in a horrible place mentally after my breakup. Now I know it was an undiagnosed depression. I felt ashamed of being a rich white tourist with all these poor Africans waiting on me. I took on a lot of guilt by association—I was bad for being a rich white imperialist American because Americans had owned slaves, treated Native Americans horribly, and cared more about money than human rights. I was bad from birth just because of the circumstances I was born into. I told my mother I was thinking about committing suicide by jumping off the roof of the Nairobi Hilton because there shouldn't even be a Nairobi Hilton! What would a normal parent say at this juncture? Maybe, "What's wrong? Let's get you some help." Maybe offer some reassurance that I was loved and wanted. Instead, she said, "Quit talking about it and do it." I asked her years later why on earth she would say something like that, and she said very dismissively, with a wave of her hand, "Oh, I was trying to call your bluff."

I lost a lot of weight while traveling, and when I returned to college, boys that wouldn't give me the time of day before treated me like I was a completely different person. I felt angry about that but also elated—now I had the upper hand. I became promiscuous, but not because I loved sex. I was just trying to prove my dad wrong—I don't look like a pig.

I got very heavily into drugs and alcohol and had an eating disorder for the next year and a half. In retrospect, I realize I was self-medicating my depression and my shame. Being thin didn't fix everything. It was preferable to be out of my head than in it. Right before the end of the first semester of my junior year, I freaked out because I was so isolated and strung out that I was afraid to turn in my term paper. I had no idea if it was brilliant or complete crap. I called my dad crying and said I wanted to come home. He said okay. And with that, I dropped out of college. No questions asked, no attempt to figure out what was going on with me, no discussion when I got home. A kid in crisis and not a parent in sight.

I call the next two years my "hell-bent on self-destruction" phase or what psychologists call a soft suicide attempt. I had absolutely no justification for taking up space, breathing air, using any resources. I was not only nothing, I wasn't even on my way to becoming something. In Econ 101, I had learned how to do a cost-benefit analysis. I kept using it on myself to see if I deserved to live, and I kept losing. I couldn't stand myself. I didn't care if I lived or died and behaved accordingly. At some point, I decided it was not even right for my parents to support me because I was twenty-one years old and didn't deserve it. Nobody else should have to pay for me. I kicked myself out and moved to another state, with a resolve to make it on my own. I did get somewhat better because I had a job and was supporting myself. I was still drinking excessively, but I always showed up for work.

Realizing I didn't want to be a waitress forever, I went to school for electronics technology. My motivation was that I'd like to work at a radio station and have access to concerts and drugs. But I ended up working in the computer industry. I went home for one month before starting my new job and met the man who would become my husband. We met at a party and had sex, but after that, he asked me out on a date! That was different.

Within a short period of time, he moved to the state where I was living, and we were together. I will never know what it was about this man, but he completely stole my heart. After living together a year and a half, we got married. A strange thing happened to me then, and I observed myself doing it: when someone at work would ask what kind of food or music or movie I liked, I would always respond with "we" and proceed to tell them what my husband liked. I was willingly giving myself away. Also, upon becoming a wife, I felt so much more pressure than being the girlfriend. Now people had the right to judge me by how clean my house was. I had standards in my mind about what makes a good wife, and I had to live up to them whether I agreed with them or not. I never really developed my own sense of what was important to me; I was way too busy trying to meet everyone else's standards (as I imagined them).

We were both daily drinkers, but now it was beer at home, not Jack Daniels at the bar. My drinking didn't get progressively worse; I didn't need to be out of my head drunk—just numb. When I found out I was pregnant (at four months), I stopped drinking and smoking immediately. What I could never do for myself, I was able to do for someone else. Of course, I started drinking again right after my son was born. I had to do fertility treatments for our second child, which turned into an eighteen-month-long period of living in shame. Having always been insecure about my femininity, here was absolute proof that I was defective as a woman.

Becoming a mother gave me a whole new set of standards I had to live up to. My life was about role-playing: be a good wife, a good mother, a good employee. Where was Beth? She didn't know herself except by these roles she let other people define for her. It's typical of shame-based people to keep up a good front and not draw attention to themselves for fear of what others may find. I wasn't totally sure what makes a good mother, but I imagined they probably didn't drink every day. I kept trying to only drink on weekends, but I could never make it that long. I didn't think I had a problem. I thought I just changed my mind.

My inability to communicate really showed up in my marriage. I thought the vows meant we were responsible for each other's happiness. So, if he was in a bad mood, it was my fault for not doing my job well enough. I never blamed him for my unhappiness though, because I never really expected much from anyone. I never allowed myself to feel anger because that would mean I didn't love him (I thought). But I *was* passive-aggressive. If I wanted him to know I was upset about something, I would only make my side of the bed and see if he could take a hint. Then, if he loved me, he should know what I was upset about. One evening, I was home making him a pie, and he called and said he was going out after work instead of coming straight home. I felt rejected, and I cut slits in the crust to allow the steam to escape that spelled F**K YOU. In retrospect, I was letting *my* steam escape. If he said something to me that struck a nerve, I would spend the rest of the day in my head with "Why did he say that? What did he mean by that? What was his motive?" I would never go back and actually say, "What do you mean by that?" It never even occurred to me; it was far too confrontational.

What Happened

After we had two kids, our marriage started deteriorating. My husband's drinking was escalating; he was having blackouts almost every night. I felt so virtuous but resentful for being the one to take care of the kids while he was out of it. I was only drinking four beers on weeknights, for which I thought I deserved a medal. He resented me for being so involved with the kids and felt abandoned. Children gave me a justification to be alive, gave me a purpose. I needed to be needed. One night he came home and told me he'd been having an affair with a coworker. After getting over the initial shock, we both agreed it was something he would not have done but for his drinking. I also knew it was because I was a bad wife. He decided to go to treatment and went to the Meadows in Wickenburg, Arizona, for six weeks.

I knew nothing about alcoholism, AA, or the Twelve Steps. I had previously told a therapist that my husband drank a twelve-pack every night but wasn't an alcoholic. When he called home from the treatment center, I asked, "Are they trying to make you believe in God?" He was a non-believer just like me but said, "Yes, they are." I told him, "They're brainwashing you. You don't need to quit; you just need to cut back. I think you should come home." Well, all hell broke loose after that. Fingers started being pointed at me, the "good" one. He couldn't come home and live with an active alcoholic who was not supportive of his recovery.

I attended his family week. I heard all the patients introducing themselves as adult children of alcoholics or dysfunctional families and felt I didn't belong there at all. When it was my turn to speak, I announced that I came from a wonderful, loving family, and if there was anything wrong with me, it was all my fault. If I had been given the

Adverse Childhood Experiences Study (ACES)[6] questionnaire at that time, I would have scored zero.

I had the shock of my life during one of the group sessions. We family members were supposed to confront our patient with specific incidents of the patient's behavior while in the throes of the disease, and tell them how it affected us. After that, the group would give feedback. I had a long list of all the things I did for him that he didn't seem to appreciate as much as I thought he should. The first feedback I got was spoken in a very negative tone of voice: "You sound like a martyr!" I thought, yes, that was one of the steps on the way to becoming a saint. When you suffer for someone, it shows how much you really love them. But here these people were making it sound like a bad thing! I was utterly baffled.

Even though they had me come back a couple of times after family week to try to convince me that I was an alcoholic too, I was still in denial. I asked the counselor if he got a commission for filling beds. Finally, I agreed to quit drinking to be supportive and to go to Al-Anon. So my sobriety date is the date he came home from treatment. I wanted more than anything to save my marriage, and I tried to follow their recommendations to the letter. I was such a deer in the headlights. They said don't do anything for the alcoholic that he can do for himself. In my mind, this meant that if I make him a sandwich and he relapses, it's my fault.

A few months later, I agreed to go to a weeklong codependency program. There, I noticed that the people who admitted to being alcoholic and were attending AA were a lot happier than people like me who were fighting to not admit it. I had another huge shock during this program: I was sitting in a group, and they were saying something I wanted to share about, so I did what you're supposed to do—put a tortured expression on your face and hope they notice. The counselor never did call on me, and somehow, afterward, I mustered up the courage to ask why. She said, "I saw you, but I was not going to enable you." What the heck was that supposed to mean? I thought enabling meant buying alcohol for an alcoholic. She said, "You were trying to get your needs met by being manipulative. You need to raise your hand and say, 'I'm hurting, and I need to share.'" I said, "Lady, you could have let me sit there for a hundred years and I never would have come up with that idea." It was on my unconscious list of things you never ever do. They also told me I needed treatment for alcohol first, even though I'd been sober for four months.

At six months sober, I went to treatment at the same place my husband had gone, The Meadows. I also participated in Pia Mellody's aftercare group for three years. I had no trouble admitting my life was unmanageable and finally admitted I was an alcoholic. Part of my holding back was that I didn't think my alcoholism was progressing; it had actually gotten better. They said I may be able to keep it at bay for a while, but when the kids are grown, it will be back. They had me do a lot of tests and diagnosed me with chemical dependency, eating disorder, and codependency. But number one on the list was something I had never heard of; it's not in the DSM, but it sure explained a lot: massive shame-based personality. (The little ego I had was kind of proud that it was massive.)

I learned I had been abused and neglected, and that I had internalized ways of coping and surviving in that environment that had become my way of being in the world. But the rest of the world was a different environment than the one I grew up in, and the things I had learned did not set me on the path for a happy, productive life with successful relationships.

Some amazing things happened there. They taught us a course that could be called Feelings 101. It was all new to me—identifying and acknowledging emotions—and it's become the foundation of my recovery. At first I thought, How could I be so stupid not to have learned such basic information by this point in my life? The answer is that at birth, I was placed in a different "school" that taught different lessons. Now I began to learn how to identify, name, and feel my feelings, and I began to learn adult-appropriate ways to deal with them.

The second thing that shocked me was this: what another person thinks, feels, says, or does, even if they're saying it about me, reveals more about them than it does about me. I had always allowed others to have a straight path into my core being. I was more inclined to believe them than myself. This is the basic concept of interpersonal boundaries. I had no defenses to anything anyone said about me. If it was bad, it was probably true. I learned that I can actually consider another person's opinion and decide how I want to respond.

I get to say who I am, not allow others to tell me who I am.

I want to shout that sentence. I grew up in a house full of funhouse mirrors, and the gaslights were on all the time. The images reflected back to me were always distorted. People were telling me I wasn't experiencing what I was experiencing. I realized that if I didn't make some major changes, I would be doing the same thing to my kids. That was a great motivator.

Here's what basically happened there. I thought I was a functional alcoholic, taking care of my responsibilities, and that's all there was to life. I had even constructed a narrative: my job was stressful because I was an engineer without an engineering degree and felt like an impostor all the time; I felt guilty about being a working mom; and I was martyring myself for my husband—so I could justify drinking every night. I was a perfect little four-cylinder engine, getting where I needed to be, meeting all my responsibilities, and drinking was my reward. But in treatment, they looked under my hood and said, "Hey, did you know you've actually got eight cylinders?" Emotion, spirituality, connection—there was more to life than being responsible.

"Functional alcoholic" is an oxymoron. All alcoholics are shut down emotionally. And my narrative was false, too. I loved my job and my kids, and my husband didn't want me to be a martyr. I was doing that to myself. I was shut down on the inside, trying to keep up appearances on the outside. Always going to the car wash, but never changing the oil or getting a tune-up. I used alcohol like turning up the radio to ignore all the noises the engine was making. I learned that I have a right to be somebody of my own making.

What It's Like Now

When I came home, I started going to AA regularly and have ever since. At first, I felt like I'd entered parallel universes—my head was analyzing everything the AA literature said and finding much of it factually incorrect, hypocritical (not allied with any sect, let's close with a Bible passage), or a blatant sales tactic (such as giving you only two options to force you to pick the one they want, when those are not really the only choices). It was screaming, get out! You don't want what they have! But my heart was pulled in the opposite direction—people talking about feelings, being honest and vulnerable, supporting one another, and not taking themselves too seriously but taking sobriety very seriously. I wanted what they had, so I stayed.

I needed to get comfortable calling my sponsor. My thinking was I'm bad if I call someone; I'm a bother. Whatever they're doing is more important than talking to me. When my sponsor told me to call her, I thought, now I'm bad if I don't call someone! I had no way of talking to myself that wasn't framed in badness of one sort or another. But I did call her and eventually learned that people do not always feel bothered when I call them. In fact, most of the time, they're happy to hear from me. An old idea changed.

Early recovery around the family was difficult. My depression came out full force. At two years sober, I was finally diagnosed, and then it took another two years to get on the right combination of anti-depressants. My relationship with my husband was emotionally volatile. I came to realize that ever since we got married, I had made him my Higher Power—if I had his approval, I didn't need everyone else's so much. One day, coming home from the grocery store, I realized I had forgotten something I was supposed to get for him. When we got home, my five-year-old son looked in the cabinet and said, "You're lucky we already had some, Mom, so Dad won't be mad at you." There it was in black and white. I had never verbalized or even been consciously aware of this behavior, but my child saw it. My worst fear was for him to be mad at me. (This might make sense if he was physically abusive, but he wasn't.)

I knew I wasn't supposed to be seeking his approval anymore, but I still couldn't stand not to have it. New behavior is uncomfortable, even if it's healthier. We disagreed on a lot of parenting issues, like many parents. He had a great fear of being a father (his father was an alcoholic), and he tried to manage his anxiety by controlling me and how I parented. I, on the other hand, was trying not to be controlled anymore and hoping for his approval in standing up for myself! I didn't have this insight at the time, of course. We were both walking wounded—shell-shocked, anxious, depressed, and struggling. But we didn't quit, and it got better.

I tried out the new ideas I had learned in treatment. My two-year-old son came to me crying because his banana broke. I didn't give him a lecture or tell him he was stupid for crying about it. I got right down to his eye level and said, "Darn that banana! We didn't want it to break, did we?" He said, "No," stopped crying, and ate his broken banana. He just needed validation. Feelings dissipate when they're expressed, but they build up when we hang onto them. We also had weekly family meetings where we talked about our feelings.

In early sobriety, my group was looking for a volunteer to take over the phone list. No one volunteered. I burst into tears because I felt so guilty and ashamed for not volunteering—if I had the ability to do something, there was no excuse for me not to do it. But with the depression and all, I didn't feel I could handle anything else at the time. Beginning to stand up for myself and my limits felt like I was committing a mortal sin. However, as I continued to practice the new behavior, I eventually got comfortable doing it. One time, in the depths of depression, I got a call from an old-timer asking me to speak at a meeting. The way I was feeling, my message would have been, "If this is what sobriety feels like, drinking was much better." So I said no. He threw a guilt trip at me about saying no to the program—how that was selfish and self-centered. But I was a person who always volunteered and did for others, and this was a rare and healthy occurrence for me to say no.

I had a big struggle in AA over the Higher Power issue. They told me I had to get one—so I tried. I tried for twenty years. I tried three different churches, for months or years at a time, and not just once or twice. I read all kinds of spiritual books. I studied anthropology, thinking that maybe there was commonality underlying all the different cultural trappings of belief systems. I got a master's degree, but still no HP. It did open my eyes to a much broader picture of what it means to be human. The *Big Book*, which preaches tolerance, doesn't really mean tolerance for all belief systems. It says if you don't believe, it's because of intellectual pride, defiance, prejudice, or vanity (thinking humans are the alpha and the omega). I felt like a bad person, a failure, an outcast, an impostor. This is the last house on the block, and I don't fit in here either; I'm even a misfit among misfits. Should I say the Lord's Prayer to fit in, or should I follow the coin that says, "To thine own self be true"?

I left many a meeting feeling worse than when I went in. People seemed to think if I didn't have a god, it meant I thought I was God. Nothing could be further from the truth. I had been willingly giving up my power to all kinds of things and people outside of myself for my whole life. Finally, after twenty years of sobriety, I thought maybe they're wrong about that—that you can't stay sober without God. I've been doing it for twenty years. I've heard people say they came to that conclusion within two or three years, but it took me that long to gain the ego strength to say that despite what everyone else believes, this is not true for me. When I was twenty-eight years sober, I met someone in the program who told me he was an atheist, sober as long as me, and he told me about a secular AA website. Turns out there were hundreds of nonbelievers in AA with decades of sobriety. Since I found secular AA, I've been much more comfortable in all AA meetings because I know I am not alone.

Another thing I had trouble with was the ego-busting. I had a very weak ego. I never tried to control people or manage them like the director in the *Big Book*. I did try to get people to like me, but that was mostly by changing me, not them. The phrase "character defects" threw me right into a shame spiral. I had known I was defective my whole life. Same with the Fourth Step—be hard on yourself, but easy on others? I'd been doing that my whole life, too. And, our constant thought must be of others? For me, it always has been because I'm codependent. Moral inventory? Now I'm not only defective but immoral!

There were so many harsh messages: "Get God or die!" "Take the cotton out of your ears and put it in your mouth." "Sit down and shut up; you don't know anything." "You are self-will run riot, selfish, and self-centered in the extreme." "If this program doesn't work for you, it's your fault. You haven't thoroughly tried." "It's your pride and ego that keep you from believing." "Look in the mirror—there's your problem!" "If the God part scares someone out, there'll be a bottle that scares them back in." And, the worst thing of all to say to someone who is suicidally depressed and feels so low about herself that she thinks the world would be better if she weren't in it: "You are getting pleasure out of this. You lack humility. This is pride in reverse. You have just as big an ego as Bill, only you think you're the worst instead of the best." That was a trigger for reliving childhood trauma—being kicked when I was down, being blindsided with reproach when I didn't even think I was doing anything wrong, because I thought I was so defective I didn't even know how defective I was.

I spent many years trying to fit myself into the personality type of the alcoholic in the *Big Book*. I didn't know who I was, so I went along with what they told me. But those words—*selfish, self-centered, egocentric*—triggered me into a massive shame response. My training said selfishness is inexcusable and to always put others' needs ahead of my own. For the most part, I had done that. And if that was all I'd heard, I would not have stayed. I stuck around because there was, besides this harshness, a feeling of love and acceptance, an atmosphere of "we don't shoot our wounded."

I love the format of AA meetings. We all admit we're not perfect, and it's okay. Meetings are a safe place to share and show emotion; no one tells me my feelings are wrong or bad or inappropriate. I kept hearing people say things I felt, but I'd never known anyone else felt that way. And there was so much laughter, but not at anyone's expense. I became a part of a community called the fellowship, and it saved me. I heard many people say they came in with a god-sized hole inside. But I came in with a Beth-sized hole. I began to build an authentic self. Before, nobody was home inside, but now, I am at home with myself. I could not have accomplished this left to my own devices, and I am thankful to the doctors, therapists, books, and especially AA for making it possible.

At around five years sober, life was good! My husband and I were proud of ourselves for the work we were doing, trying to break the cycles of abuse and alcoholism in our families. Our marriage was strong. We didn't go to the same meetings, which was good for me because it allowed me to be a standalone person, not just his partner. I did lots of self-esteem work, listening to affirmations and trying to eliminate my negative self-talk. I used to think I would never accomplish anything if I stopped beating myself up, but I learned through experience that positive motivation really works better for me. I kept my distance from my parents for a while—until I could build up boundaries and not allow them to *zing* me out of the blue.

One day, when we were about six and a half years sober, my husband woke up with a headache. It kept getting worse, so we went to the emergency room. It turned out he had a brain bleed from an aneurysm and needed emergency brain surgery. He was never the same again. After some time, he resembled how he used to look physically, but his frontal lobes were damaged, and he had trouble with impulse control, initiation, motivation, and judgment. For a couple years there, our family was more dysfunctional than when we were drinking. He got into physical fights with the kids, deliberately embarrassed them in public because he thought it was funny, and was hit or miss on giving the kids appropriate instructions. It was so confusing to them as to when they should do what Dad said and when they should not. Now, instead of two adults and two kids, it was one adult and three kids.

After two years, we separated because I had done all I could for him and it wasn't safe for the kids. Hardest choice I ever had to make and try not to feel guilty about! After five years, I divorced him, and that was my second hardest choice. I realized that I was still putting most of my emotional energy into him and his issues, not seeing any positive results, and ignoring my own.

I was trying to keep so many plates spinning, I made a conscious choice to let go of something. I stopped watching what I ate. Over the next few years, I gained fifty pounds. My stinking thinking said, "You're not sober. You just switched addictions. You might as well drink." Fortunately, my friends in the program reminded me that I wouldn't get arrested for fat driving or open containers of Twinkies, or have my kids taken away from me for being overweight. That was the only time in my whole adult life that I was actually fat. And, it was the only period in my life when I didn't worry twenty to fifty times a day if I was getting fat—because I knew I was. My earlier worries had been caused by my distorted body image and unrealistic standards.

At some point, my ex-husband picked up drinking again and proceeded to drink himself to death. He couldn't cope with not being who he used to be and didn't understand why he couldn't work or why the kids didn't want to be around him. I stayed close to him the whole time—took him grocery shopping, to doctors' appointments, invited him for holidays. I still felt intensely loyal to him because I knew who he had been. He was kicked out of every rehab for smoking in his room and told not to come back to the hospital because he was non-compliant. He simply couldn't follow rules because of the brain injury. It took him ten years to die, and it was horrible to watch.

As I look back on that experience, awful as it was, it forced me to take charge, be the decision-maker. I had to be an advocate for him, had to speak up. I might still be living in his shadow if I hadn't been forced out. During that time, I cleared away the wreckage of my past, education-wise. I finished my bachelor's degree and got a master's degree in anthropology. Then I went to law school and worked as a public defender for my second career. Now I had to advocate for my clients. I worked in an adversarial system and learned how to handle conflict. I felt a real sense of purpose in that job, that I was doing something worthwhile. It was good for my self-esteem. These experiences helped me become an advocate for myself when necessary, too.

Thanks to AA, after many years, I became fairly comfortable in my own skin, except, ironically, in AA meetings—until I met other secular sober people. I am not the same personality type that Bill believed applied to all alcoholics. I thought too little— not too much—of myself. I focused on the needs and wants of others, rather than my own. I had no sense of entitlement. I did not seek your praise and admiration; I just hoped you'd tolerate me as long as I didn't bother you. That's why I'm writing this book—to help others like me build, not destroy, their self-esteem. I hope AA won't be as uncomfortable for you after reading this.

2

SOME DEFINITIONS

Boundaries

A boundary is simply a line separating two things. In this book, we are talking about inter-personal boundaries—physical, emotional, sexual, mental, and spiritual. Boundaries exist for two purposes: to prevent us from invading the space of others and to prevent others from invading our space. When someone steps on my foot, they violate my physical boundary. It's not my fault for being in their way. Boundaries are flexible, and we can have different boundaries with different people. For example, being raped invades my sexual boundary but consensual sex does not.

Many of us do not know exactly where we end and the next person begins. We take on the feelings of others, or we may blame them for causing our feelings. When I have a healthy boundary with someone, I can allow them to have their thoughts, opinions, and feelings without taking them on as my own, and I can have my own thoughts, opinions, and feelings *without apology because I have the same right they do.* Another boundary area concerns responsibility—what is mine to do and what is not mine to do. I am responsible for my behavior, my decisions, my recovery. I cannot be responsible for yours. Many of us like to think we are helping when we take responsibility for another's problems, but we are actually enabling them to continue their irresponsible behavior by protecting them from the consequences.

Al-Anon is immensely helpful in forming boundaries.

- He is angry; must I be? No, he can have his feelings, and I can have mine.

- She's too hungover to go to work or even call in. Should I call her boss and say she has the flu? No, her job is her responsibility.

- He blames me for everything. That is his own pain coming out. I will not take on any guilt that is not mine.

You will find countless examples of what Al-Anon calls detaching, even detaching with love. It's possible to live with and love difficult people when we have boundaries. Once I stopped trying to get emotional support from my mother, who doesn't know how to give it, our relationship improved. Stop going to the hardware store for grapefruit! Find someone else who *can* give you emotional support. Also, don't be surprised when fig trees bear figs. Mom or Dad may zing me out of the blue on any given occasion, but I will not let it hurt me because I'm half expecting it, and it's really more about who they are than who I am. It's easier to wear shoes than to carpet the world.

Egomaniac personalities tend to cross over other people's boundaries, and those of us with low self-worth tend not to defend our own boundaries. It's said in the rooms that alcoholics don't have relationships—they take hostages. Some of us also give ourselves up to be hostages. We latch onto someone else's life instead of creating our own.

One time, going into marriage counseling with my husband, the therapist asked, "How are you feeling today, Beth?" I responded, "He's mad at me." She said, "But how are *you* doing?" I thought I had answered her. She should know that when he's mad at me, I'm in the doghouse feeling shame and walking on eggshells. Bad therapist! I was displaying a lack of emotional boundary and taking my cue from his feelings to determine my feelings.

Codependency

Originally, codependency was narrowly applied to the behaviors adopted by a person in a relationship with an addict or alcoholic. Today, the definition has expanded to a set of personality traits common in people from dysfunctional families. It's is a learned behavior that can be passed down from one generation to another. It involves emotional and behavioral characteristics that affect an individual's ability to have healthy, mutually satisfying relationships.[7]

People with codependency often form or maintain relationships that are one-sided and emotionally destructive and/or abusive out of fear of abandonment. "Codependents have low self-esteem and look for anything outside of themselves to make them feel better. They find it hard to 'be themselves.' Some try to feel better through alcohol, drugs, or nicotine and become addicted. Others may develop compulsive behaviors like workaholism, gambling, or indiscriminate sexual activity."[8]

Codependents tend to see themselves as good people who care about others, but the "caring" is often self-abandonment to focus on the needs of others in an attempt to feel valued or secure because codependents don't know their own worth. The pamphlet *Am I Codependent?* on the Codependents Anonymous website describes more characteristics and behaviors of codependents.[9]

Many codependents are caretakers because they were forced into that position in their family or rewarded for doing it. I cried when I didn't want to volunteer for the phone list because I had internalized that if something needs to be done, I am supposed to do it. Otherwise, there's no excuse for me. Not volunteering was lazy, selfish, and irresponsible. I felt so much shame at that moment for not raising my hand, even though no one else seemed to. AA's emphasis that we have all been takers and now it's time to give is not the right message for us. Many of us have been compulsive givers. People have described me as being "generous to a fault." Probably trying to give away my shameful silver spoon.

Codependents may be so overly concerned about the feelings of others that they neglect their own needs. Here's a silly example: I'm waiting to make a right turn out of a parking lot. If I go right now, the person coming down the street will have time to see me and slow down, but if he has to slow down, he might be mad at me. Now someone is behind me, waiting for me to go. If I wait for the first guy, I'll be holding up the guy behind me and he might be mad at me. Panic! I can't win! I don't imagine Bill W. found himself in this kind of predicament. There is no part of this decision that needs to involve the imagined feelings of total strangers.

All the lines in popular music —like I'm nothing without you; I can't live without you; you're my everything; you're my reason to live; you treat me so bad I love you even more; I'd do anything to keep you; please don't leave me, I'll be lost—are all about codependent, not healthy, relationships. If you want to see the difference between making another person your Higher Power versus God, google the lyrics to Celine Dion's song "Because You Loved Me" (songwriter Diane Warren), put it in the present tense, and imagine it both ways.

Here are some dynamics of codependent relationships, which may be operating without any awareness on our part:

1. I don't have any value unless you approve of me all the time.

2. I only feel good about myself when I'm taking care of others, so I will find someone who is needy or welcomes my enabling.

3. I fear both intimacy and abandonment, so I will find someone who is the same way, and we will be forever getting too close, breaking up, feeling abandoned, and getting back together till we feel too close again.

Two great books on codependency are *Codependent No More* (Beatty, 1986) and *Facing Codependence* (Mellody, 1989).

Ego

The common definition of ego is simply "your idea or opinion of yourself, especially your feeling of your own importance and ability."[10] It's not good or bad, and we don't get rid of it. I agree with Bill that we need to get "right-sized." But his assumption is that all alcoholics have inflated egos and that getting "right-sized" means getting off your high horse. Some of us come in riding donkeys or walking or crawling, and we need to get a horse. The Twelve Steps work for both types because they help us take an honest look at ourselves and fix what needs fixing.

In psychology, there is another definition of ego, first conceived by Freud, as being the part of ourselves that mediates between the id (base instincts) and the superego (conscience). Bill W. talks a lot about our instincts and says they serve a purpose—for us to eat, drink, belong, reproduce, seek security, etc.—but that in alcoholics these instincts go beyond their original purpose to the point where we demand that people supply us with these things. This implies that the id is running our lives and we need *more* ego. Since he doesn't explain which definition he is using, it's very confusing.

To keep things simple, I'm sticking with the first definition. But I disagree with the saying heard in the rooms that "My ego is not my amigo." A grandiose ego is not my amigo. Neither is a shattered one. We are all striving for a realistic, healthy sense of self.

Self

The self, in the sense that I am using it, is "the union of elements (such as body, emotions, thoughts, and sensations) that constitute the individuality and identity of a person."[11] When I first read that definition, I thought, boy, I need to get me one of those. Imagine being a unified whole person! Synonyms for self are personality, nature, character, identity, and ego. Some people have a strong sense of self, and some people have a weak sense of self.

A strong sense of self means a realistic perception of all these parts of ourselves, ownership of them, and the ability to integrate them. It means there is somebody home inside, not a hole that we try to fill with other things. We have a secure base from which we can head out and to which we can return. We don't have to compartmentalize our experiences or live in constant cognitive dissonance.

How would you know when you're off-kilter if you don't know where your kilter is?

An over or underdeveloped sense of self is usually the result of emotional abuse and neglect. We don't see ourselves accurately. Bill inaccurately perceived himself as greater and more powerful than he was. We often tend to see ourselves as smaller than we are. We don't trust our thoughts; we repress and don't own our emotions; we often have a distorted body-image; we give away our power; and we don't form any kind of union of our different parts. My recovery journey has been about growing into a stronger sense of self.

The *Big Book* has a lot of negative things to say about the self, but I think what Bill is talking about is his preoccupation with his own needs, wants, and ambitions without regard for others. That's one aspect of self, but not the one we who have an underdeveloped sense of self struggle with. We tend to have too much regard for others and not enough for ourselves.

Self-will is not a bad thing either. I will myself to get out of bed in the morning. I will myself to go to work. Even when I pray for God's will, it's my will doing the praying. It's self-will run riot, or willfulness, that's the problem—trying to exercise our will over people, places, and things we have no ability or authority to control, or rampaging like a bull in a china shop without regard to the damage we're causing. This is the beast Bill is trying to tame, the power driver, but not all of us have it.

3

A BRIEF HISTORY OF THE AA PROGRAM

The original AA members were low-bottom drunks who had been try-ing to get sober for a long time. Dr. Bob had been attending Oxford Group meetings for two and a half years before he met Bill. It wasn't keeping him sober. Bill had dried out several times but couldn't stay stopped. That "I've got this!" feeling always came back. In Bill's descrip-tions of himself, there is some foreshadowing of his personality type before he ever became an alcoholic. In *AA Comes of Age*, he tells the story about making a boomerang when he was a kid.[12] At age ten, he was awkward and gangly and got pushed around by smaller kids. He decided that instead of being depressed about this, he was going to win at all costs. His grandfather told him that no one could make and throw a boomerang except an Australian bushman. It took him six months, but he succeeded. He wanted the recognition of being the first man in America to do it. And he described those six months as being on a "power drive."

Bill went on to describe the attitude toward life that he adopted. He had to be the first, the best, the winner at everything in order to avoid a deep-seated feeling of inferiority. Unwilling to settle for sec-ond-rate status, he vowed to dominate in everything he did. His whole life was a power drive. In his *Big Book* story, during the war he received a special note of appreciation from the men in his battery. In his mind, that was confirmation of his enormous talent that would lead him to become a giant in industry, running multiple large companies (grandiosity). When he started competing in golf, he had a role for Lois, too—to watch and applaud (other people are props to make him look good).

He talks a lot in Step Twelve in the *Twelve & Twelve* about this personality type's strategy for dealing with feelings of inferiority: to win, dominate, collect accolades, and demand from others that they acknowledge his superiority. One author describes the development of the narcissistic personality this way: "It's such an old story. A neglected boy must play-act as manly to win his father's approval. And he does it so well that, eventually, the costume just becomes his clothes and then, finally, his skin."[13] In Bill's case, this tendency wasn't related to his father, but the persona he adopted as a defense mechanism eventually became the person he was—impenetrable, unable to admit defeat, closed-minded, on rare occasions aware that he wasn't really as good as he made himself out to be, and drunk. In Step Seven in the *Twelve & Twelve*, he talks about his complete aversion to humility and how hard it is to overcome.

In Bill's *Big Book* story, after his old friend Ebby came to visit him and was sober for the first time in years, attributing it to religion, Bill described himself as choking or gagging on the idea of a power greater than himself. Yet, shortly after his white light experience, he was telling people he was going to sober up all the drunks on the planet (more grandiosity).[14]

These are Bill's own descriptions of himself. I am not a psychologist and would not attempt to diagnose him. However, his contemporary, psychiatrist Dr. Harry Tiebout, who worked with him and some of the other early AA members, did just that. He said the typical alcoholic personality was narcissistic and egocentric, and his main character traits are defiance and grandiosity. He believes himself to be omnipotent and cannot easily accept the idea of God. The feeling of superiority must be maintained at all costs. No one can tell him what to do because he knows better than everyone else. The presence of a God challenges the very nature of the alcoholic.[15] (Ask yourself, does this sound like me? Do I see myself as omnipotent?) For Bill, the acceptance of a power greater than himself was a huge shift in personality, a "psychic change." From there, the alcoholic begins to accept help and is on his way. Describing one of the early members who had undergone a "psychological awakening," Dr. Tiebout noted that his façade had been pierced, his defenses had stopped working. He used to view himself as the all-powerful center of the universe, and other people only mattered in how they affected him. He had been completely unaware that other people had their own separate lives, different from his. He now realized he was just a small part of a huge world.[16]

The need for a Higher Power to stay sober came about because of this personality type. They needed to admit they were not God. (I've always found it amusing that I could find any number of powers greater than me just by looking around the room or out the window, but to be higher than Bill saw himself, this power needed to be omnipotent.) I suspect the early members were low-bottom precisely because their narcissism told them never to admit defeat. Surrender was not an option. That's why Bill and Bob tried to sober up drunks who were hospitalized—to catch them at their weakest. Then they *might* be able to admit defeat. In addition to admitting they were not God, the other thing that really helped them was one alcoholic talking to another. As power drivers, they had never felt a real, human-level connection with another person, whether due to their alcoholism or narcissism. But they could relate to each other as alcoholics. Connecting with others is the cornerstone of many people's recovery, and it's the part of AA that saved me.

The descriptions of the alcoholic personality in the *Big Book* reflect this particular set of alcoholics—playing God, arranging the scenery, directing the show, all without taking into account any other person's feelings or even acknowledging that other people have their own wants, needs, plans, and desires that may be different from their own. The AA program was designed to crush this egomania, self-centeredness, grandiosity, and lack of regard for others. The Twelve Steps for ego deflation worked for these people. It helped them, and it has helped millions of other alcoholics like them. Unfortunately, as so easily happens with small, homogeneous, self-selected samples, two factors—egomaniac personality type and alcoholism—were conflated. Compounding this error, the extrapolation from a small number of early AA members to a universal alcoholic personality type went too far. Now we know that there are alcoholics who are not egomaniacs and there are egomaniacs who are not alcoholics.

Because they had the brilliant idea to share their stories in the *Big Book*, many readers began to see that their drinking was headed on the same trajectory, so they did not have to hit as low of a bottom. They didn't have an issue with admitting their need for help and came into the program sooner. All kinds of personalities found a home in AA, not only narcissists. Many of us suffer the same sense of inferiority that Bill did but did not develop the same defense to it; Bill became an egomaniac, while we just lived with feeling inferior. Our soul sickness lies in feeling not worthy of God, rather than thinking we are God. Our egos need building, not crushing.

One thing we have in common is a lack of insight into our true nature. Another is the goal to remain sober and become a principled and authentic human being. The Twelve Steps provide a clear outline of how to attain these goals. There is tremendous value in doing them. We need some sort of structure upon which to build our new life. The Twelve Steps are not the only way, maybe not even the best way. But they are a proven method, and besides providing the Steps, AA provides a therapeutic environment where we can work on ourselves with love and support, and sponsorship so that we have someone to guide us through this unfamiliar territory.

One of the goals of sobriety is to be true to ourselves. The harder I tried to conform myself to the description of the alcoholic in the book, the less true I was being to myself. It was no different from my parents telling me who I was, what I thought, how I felt. That was not recovery for me.[17] In AA, I learned to develop an inner, secure sense of who I am, but it was not easy because the program was not designed for me. This book will offer some adaptations to the original program that can prevent us from going into shame and focus more on strengthening our sense of self rather than further crushing what is already crushed.

4
EGOMANIACS AND SHAME-BASED PEOPLE

There is a whole spectrum of degrees in how people see themselves. On the low end, some see themselves as utterly worthless and undeserving of life, love, or happiness. Further up, there are people with low self-esteem but not to the point of questioning their right to exist. There's just that nagging feeling of not being enough—not smart enough, not good enough, not man enough. There are people toward the middle who know they are competent in some areas but have the feeling of not being enough in other areas. There are people who accept themselves as they are, with a realistic assessment of themselves and a sense of being "good enough," even when they make mistakes. That's healthy. Above that, we have people who think they are pretty great, minus a few insignificant shortcomings. Then we have people like Bill, with many narcissistic traits but not impervious to change. At the top is narcissistic personality disorder (NPD), which is incurable. Nothing can penetrate the person's defenses.

In *Rethinking Narcissism*,[18] Craig Malkin describes this spectrum, identifies some traits as "healthy narcissism," and has a test you can take to see where you fall on the spectrum.[19] Here, I'm using the word "egomaniac" (AA language) interchangeably with "narcissist" (psychology language).

What Does it Mean to Be a Narcissist?

The Mayo Clinic website offers a comprehensive description:[20]

- Have an exaggerated sense of self-importance
- Have a sense of entitlement and require constant, excessive admiration
- Expect to be recognized as superior even without achievements that warrant it
- Exaggerate achievements and talents
- Be preoccupied with fantasies about success, power, brilliance, beauty, or the perfect mate
- Believe they are superior and can only associate with equally special people
- Monopolize conversations and belittle or look down on people they perceive as inferior
- Expect special favors and unquestioning compliance with their expectations
- Take advantage of others to get what they want
- Have an inability or unwillingness to recognize the needs and feelings of others
- Be envious of others and believe others envy them
- Behave in an arrogant or haughty manner, coming across as conceited, boastful, and pretentious
- Insist on having the best of everything—for instance, the best car or office
- Become impatient or angry when they don't receive special treatment
- Have significant interpersonal problems and easily feel slighted

- React with rage or contempt and try to belittle the other person to make themselves appear superior
- Have difficulty regulating emotions and behavior
- Experience major problems dealing with stress and adapting to change
- Feel depressed and moody because they fall short of perfection
- Have secret feelings of insecurity, shame, vulnerability, and humiliation

These are all a matter of degree, and people may have some of the characteristics but not others.

Bill also talks about the flip side of his narcissism. Psychologists call this the narcissistic wound. He calls it self-centered fear, which sounds something like shame. He talks about his dependencies on people, places, and things and how he sinks into this flip side when they fail to prop up his ego. When he's not the best, he thinks he's the worst and wallows in self-pity. In Step Four in the *Twelve & Twelve*, he says we get a painful pleasure from our self-loathing, and that this is pride in reverse—we have lost all humility.

This manifestation of shame is nothing like mine. I don't wallow in self-pity. "Why me?" implies that I think I deserve better—entitlement. I did not get any pleasure out of self-loathing. The idea that this is somehow prideful—except we take pride in being the worst instead of the best—is damaging to people like me. I have seen many people latch onto this description when they don't relate to the egomaniac personality, since it is the only alternative offered. All it does is give us a new way to question our reality (I must be in denial about enjoying this) and beat ourselves up for being prideful in reverse. It's important to see there are different manifestations of feeling low self-worth, and we do not have to try to fit ourselves into Bill's mold.

What Does it Mean to Be Shame-Based?

In *The Psychology of Shame*, Gershen Kaufman defines the feeling of shame as "to feel seen in a painfully diminished sense. Shame reveals the inner self, exposing it to view... To feel shame is to feel inherently bad, fundamentally flawed as a person."[21] He describes it as feeling naked before an audience, unmasked, so that everyone knows you're an impostor. Self-consciousness is a manifestation of shame, a fear of exposure. We can even feel ashamed of our shame, as when we try to hide our blushing. I shuddered watching *Schindler's List* when the women were being driven to the "showers," but it was because I'd hate for them to see me naked; then I felt ashamed of having that thought given the circumstances and beat myself up for being self-centered. I occasionally experience shame about still having shame after all these years of working on it, because I think I should be better by now. But I *am* better now. You just can't erase the past completely.

Beverly Engel, in *Healing Your Emotional Self*, describes shame as "a feeling deep within us of being exposed and unworthy. When we feel ashamed, we want to hide. We hang our heads, stoop our shoulders, and curve inward as if trying to make ourselves invisible."[22] I vividly remember the hot flush on my face and the tears while being forced to write "I am a dumbbell."

Brené Brown defines shame as "the intensely painful feeling or experience of believing that we are flawed and therefore unworthy of love and belonging."[23]

Shame carries with it the fear of exposure. We don't want others to see us for who we really (think we) are. We wear masks and put on acts and feel like impostors, or we remain aloof and don't reveal anything about ourselves, or we lash out when we feel exposed. Those of us who believe we are not enough are afraid you will confirm it, so we hide it.

Shame is different from guilt. Guilt is about something I did wrong or failed to do when I should have. Guilt arises over specific things. It is forgivable, often fixable. Being shame-based is something a person feels all the time, at least on some level. It's about who I am, not what I did, and I'm irredeemable.

Egomaniac vs. Shame-Based Tendencies

The table below highlights some differences between the two personality types. See which one you identify with more, and you will know if this book is for you. You may not identify with either. I'm not trying to force anyone into a false dichotomy, nor am I saying all alcoholics fall into these two categories. And many people will recognize some of themselves on both sides.

Egomaniac Tendencies	Shame-based Tendencies
Sense of entitlement; expect special treatment and compliance with their demands.	Feel unentitled, undeserving, unworthy; leave the good stuff for someone else.
Take what they want, assuming it's deserved.	Don't even ask for what they want; assume they don't deserve it.
Seek praise from others to validate an inflated sense of self; "I'd prove to the world that I was important." (Bill's story)	Also seek outside validation, either to try to prove to themselves they're minimally acceptable or as a substitute for feeling valuable from within.

Love praise. Can't handle criticism; it means they're wrong, and they can't be wrong.	Like praise but secretly don't believe it, or can't handle praise or attention and usually deflect it; can't handle criticism either because it triggers a shame reaction.
Unaware of other people's feelings; use others as supporting cast where they are the star.	Are very tuned in to other people's feelings but oblivious to their own.
Self-centered; the world revolves around them.	Other-centered. Focus on what others may think of them, not on how they see themselves. Need to do for others so they don't feel like a burden.
Create the egomaniac false self to avoid conscious or unconscious feelings of inferiority.	Create false personas or wear many masks that look good on the outside to prevent others from seeing the (believed) ugliness within, and stick with their feelings of inferiority.
Behavior is driven largely by the defense mechanism of "I'm the best" to avoid the feeling of "I'm the worst."	Behavior is driven by internalized feelings of shame, being unworthy, not enough, defective, unlovable.
Although they long for adulation, they don't really care about what people think except for that. Think they know better than others.	Care way too much about what others might think. Hypervigilant because fearful of attack or unmasking by others—being exposed for who they believe they really are. Want everyone's approval.

Don't ask for help because they think they don't need it; would be an admission of weakness.	Don't ask for help because they don't want to bother anyone; hate to impose themselves on others.
Always have to be right. Unable to accept other people's point of view. A different opinion feels like an attack—they're saying I'm wrong—and that can't be allowed.	Point of view often depends on whose approval is needed at the moment. Or may have an opinion but will not express it in order to avoid conflict.
Always want more—driven by the need to succeed, to top others, anything that feeds the ego.	Never feel like they've done enough or are enough, even in the face of great accomplishments.
Don't respect authority because they know better. Defiant.	Need approval from or want to please authority figures. Compliant.
Come off as very sure of themselves.	Constantly second-guess themselves as to what they really think or feel or how they should have done better. Lack a solid sense of self.
Confrontation is an opportunity to win.	Confrontation is terrifying, for the most part. But sometimes lash out at people who they think are about to expose them.
Enter a new scene or situation and immediately try to dominate the conversation.	Hang back for a good while until they get a feel for how to fit in.
Love to draw attention to themselves.	Being the center of attention is very uncomfortable—fear of exposure as a fraud, failure, loser.

Play God; think they are God. All-powerful.	Give their power away to others to determine how they feel about themselves or what kind of day they will have. Do not feel the least bit omnipotent.
Brag about accomplishments, often taking more credit than due.	Don't recognize their accomplishments, or minimize them, or give the credit to someone else.
Blame others when things go wrong. It's not me; it's you.	Blame themselves for everything, even things outside their control. Accept responsibility for the wrongdoing of others. It's not you; it's me.
Do nothing for others unless it's part of a self-aggrandizement scheme.	Constantly do for others—other people's needs come first.
Lack empathy. Unable to see the world from another person's point of view.	Have tons of empathy for others but very little compassion for themselves.

Table 1. Comparison of Egomaniac and Shame-based Tendencies

If you are more like the first column, the AA program was designed for you, and I wish you well in your sobriety. If you are more like the second column, come with me on the journey I've taken, learning how to use the program to build up my strength of character, improve my self-esteem, and avoid getting triggered by some of the shaming messages in AA literature in the process.

5

WHAT DOES CHILDHOOD HAVE TO DO WITH LOW SELF-ESTEEM?

What Happened in Our Childhoods

Before we get into this, I want to emphasize three important points:

1. The purpose of looking at what happened to us is not to assign blame. The purpose is to take a realistic look at what we've been through and how it has shaped us. We are doing it for the sake of our own recovery, for which we take full responsibility.

2. I am not saying our caregivers were bad people. Many of them were "adult children" too—children of alcoholics, addicts, bullies, narcissists, etc. They didn't know any better, so they couldn't do any better. They couldn't transmit what they didn't have. Some situations were out of their control—poverty, mental illness, or disability, for example. They had their struggles just like we do. If you are a parent, ask yourself, "Did I suddenly become all-knowing and infallible the day my first child was born?" We just need to see them as ordinary humans, no different from us, and not keep them on the pedestal they had when we were younger.

3. For those of you who feel guilty about raising kids while in active alcoholism, please do not beat yourself up. If you could have done better, you would have. You were not taught the skills of healthy self-esteem and how to pass them on. You were taught to stuff your feelings, put on a good but inauthentic face, and internalize the devalued feeling that comes from being told that who you really are is not acceptable. How could you possibly have come from that and done things any differently? It's never too late to share with your kids what you are learning now. You are setting a great example by showing that change is possible and it's okay to ask for help.

"All happy families are alike; every unhappy family is unhappy in its own way."[24] There are countless ways for families to be dysfunctional.[25] Happy families are open, honest, expressive, and nurturing. Each person has a secure place that has not been predefined by someone else but instead allows the individual freedom to grow, learn, and self-define. Children know they are loved even when they misbehave, make mistakes, or act their age. They are not only allowed to have feelings but taught how to manage them. The adults behave like adults and are good role models. The CDC-Kaiser Permanente Adverse Childhood Experiences (ACE) Study was one of the largest investigations ever conducted on childhood abuse and neglect and its effects on children's health and well-being later in life.[26] One of the study's conclusions:

> Safe, stable, nurturing relationships and environments are essential to prevent early adversity, including child abuse and neglect, and to assure that all children reach their full potential.[27]

The *Spiritual Experience* appendix to the *Big Book* stresses that the alcoholic must undergo a psychic change to recover from alcoholism. Our most basic sense of who we are is formed in childhood. We internalize all sorts of messages from our main caretakers even before we are verbal. When a baby cries and no one comes, eventually the baby doesn't even bother crying. When a baby is handled roughly, he learns to associate fear and pain with human contact. When the mother has a look of contempt or disgust on her face while tending to the baby, the baby learns that she is contemptible or disgusting. A look of annoyance—I must be a bother. Being yelled at for crying—I'm not supposed to feel bad, something's wrong with me, I must hide it from them. When a child expresses a feeling and is told to just stop it and that it's wrong to feel that way, he thinks he is bad for having feelings and learns to repress them. Or she's told she should feel a different way—what's wrong with me that I don't have the right feeling? When a young child is bullied and tells a parent, and the parent offers no comfort, reassurance, or instruction—it must be okay for people to bully me.

We are forming our beliefs about ourselves in the world, although we are not aware of it. Who am I? Do I belong? Do I matter? Is it safe? Can I trust anyone? Is there enough to go around? Who gets what? Will anyone help me? Am I lovable, worthy, adequate? When I went to codependency treatment and was told to raise my hand and say, "I'm hurting and I need to share," I never would have come up with that solution. It was firmly ingrained in me not to show feelings or ask for anything that wasn't material and easily given. I was not even aware I had that "rule" inside of me or that there were alternatives. When I attended an AA retreat led by a Catholic priest, he said the big question is, "Do you feel welcome in the world or not?" That took zero pondering on my part—absolutely not! Children from healthy families know they are loved, wanted, accepted for who they are, without question.

Without discounting the role that genetics plays in personality, which may be considerable, no one is born a narcissist or feeling less-than, as far as I know.[28] A new-born baby is almost always perceived as a precious new life. When did we stop being precious? Something happened to us. We did not at some point become defective or not enough. We came to *believe* we were defective or not enough. I knew this for sure by the time I was five. The wonderful news here is that since this is learned, we can change it!

People are generally aware of overt abuse but may be completely unaware they were emotionally or spiritually abused or neglected. That was me at my husband's family week—completely clueless about the reality of my family. The reason we aren't aware is because as children we don't have anything to compare it to. Until I read *The Emotionally Absent Mother*, I had no idea what I'd been missing out on.[29] I only had the mother I had, and I didn't know that other mothers offered more. I thought Mom and Dad were fine and I was bad.

When the same person teaches you to brush your teeth, look before crossing the street, there's no excuse for you, pick your clothes up, don't cry, don't get angry, do your homework, shame on you, don't tease your sister, pick up your toys, etc., it all gets kind of jumbled together, and a lot of it appears sensible. We have no way to sort out what's true or healthy and what's not. Here's a trivial example: One time when I was a kid, I heard my mother comment that she would not want to live in a house on a corner, because you have that side yard you have to take care of but you can't really use it for anything. Fast forward to looking at houses for myself with a realtor, and she points out the one I ended up buying saying, "This one's on a corner, so that's a plus." Because I had some recovery, instead of thinking to myself I better find a new realtor, I asked, "How is that a plus?" She said, "Well, because you don't have a neighbor on one side." I was still going by what my mother taught me without ever reexamining it till then. There will be a lot of reexamining to do as our unconscious "rules" pop up during recovery.

Dysfunctional families are not the only breeding grounds for low self-esteem. A child can feel rejected because of race, gender, ethnicity, poverty, adoption, or disability, for example. Being bullied or teased, moving around a lot, having a sibling who requires lots of extra attention—many factors can contribute to a person's low self-worth. But the people who have the most contact with us when we are very young are the ones who have the biggest effect on what we internalize as our brains are developing.[30] They are also the ones who could mitigate the harm caused by other factors.

A lot of this internalizing happens before we are even verbal. Our brains are still forming and making new neural connections at a rapid pace from birth through childhood. The more repetition, the stronger the connection.[31] Many neural connections are about associations—neurons that fire together wire together. Some experiences are associated with pain or fear, some with pleasure, some with shame. Since many of our experiences, even preverbal, are linked to pain, fear, and shame, our brains become literally wired that way, and that is how we react to new experiences of a similar nature.

One of the more obvious abuses is being told we were wrong from birth—you were supposed to be a boy, you were supposed to be a tough guy, you were supposed to be petite and pretty like your mother, you were born with a silver spoon in your mouth, we didn't want any more children, I wish I hadn't knocked up your mother, having kids ruined my life. We can feel these attitudes toward us without knowing words to describe them. This is all blaming the child for nothing the child did or could have done differently. These are immature parents who haven't dealt with their own baggage passing their issues on to their children. Children are helpless to defend themselves against statements like these and begin to feel bad, unworthy, unlovable. Of course, this can continue throughout childhood when children are not fulfilling their parents' needs and dreams. These parents have it backward—parents are supposed to take care of their children's needs, not the other way around. Children have their own dreams and are not here to complete the parents' missing spaces so the parent can feel good.

When I say spiritual abuse, I am not talking about a deity. I'm talking about the spark of life we are born with, "this little light of mine," our essence or uniqueness. When we are punished for having it, instead of guided in healthy ways to express it, that little light is all but snuffed out. Along with it goes joy, exuberance, and spontaneity—soon to be replaced by depression and anxiety. It's easy to see how alcohol fits in this scenario. It helps numb the feelings we aren't allowed to own or express, calms our social anxiety, relieves our crippling self-consciousness, quiets the relentless critic in our heads, and it may be the only way we can have fun.

If our caregivers are unable, unwilling, or uninterested in allowing us to be ourselves, don't see our uniqueness as worthwhile and of value, and don't provide time, attention, direction, and nurturing to help us become our best selves, we are pretty much left to our own devices to figure a way to fit in with what they want and deal with the emotional pain of the loss of our true selves.

Having an alcoholic or addict parent is considered an adverse childhood experience.[32] Many alcoholics had an alcoholic parent who may have been Bill's personality type. They cannot help but see their children as extensions of themselves rather than independent beings. Their unfulfilled hopes and dreams are pushed onto the child to fulfill. And the negative aspects of their own personalities, which they can't bear to see or acknowledge, are also projected onto the child. Every time I asked my mom for something and she said I was lazy, selfish, and irresponsible, that's exactly what she was being. I also think she was full of self-loathing, but rather than owning it, she projected it onto me. It was like a commandment: Thou shalt not feel good about thyself. *Trapped in the Mirror: Adult Children of Narcissists in Their Struggle for Self* covers this topic quite well.[33] I don't know if my mother was a narcissist, but I related to most of the character traits of the adult children. One is having difficulty owning our reality. We were too often told this is what you think; this is how you feel; you want this, not that; you can't possibly believe that, when we thought we did. This is the house full of funhouse mirrors where the gaslights are on all the time.

After I'd been sober a few years, I mentioned to my mother a book about grandchildren of alcoholics. She said, "Don't bother reading it. I already did and you don't relate to it." I would never call in sick unless I had a fever because I couldn't be sure if I was really sick or faking it due to some unconscious motive that only my mother was capable of discerning. I will never forget the delight I felt in hanging a bird feeder, seeing a bird I didn't recognize, and finding it in a book that confirmed my observation. Validation—I really did see exactly what I thought I saw! I was forty years old.

Perhaps a parent cared a lot about status or keeping up with the Joneses. We learned to constantly compare and judge. Perhaps we were frequently compared to kids from other families. My dad wanted us girls to be more like the girls in a different family who were cute and flirty. Our mom would never have allowed that. Perhaps a parent freely criticized and called out mistakes but said nothing when everything was all right. We did not learn to give ourselves credit for anything. We may have become perfectionists to avoid the criticism. Perhaps we were only valued when we were taking care of others, including the parents, so we became caretakers who feel good about ourselves only when we're doing for others. We also think we are being good and valuable in caring for others, when we may actually be enabling or crossing people's boundaries. We carry these lessons around with us into adulthood, always putting ourselves down or feeling like we came up short (again!), telling ourselves we are not enough or that we are only enough when we live up to certain standards that are usually a lot higher than we'd expect of anyone else. Somehow, we're supposed to be different from the way we are.

Children know they are dependent on their parents for survival. A baby is supposed to form an attachment bond with its main caregiver, usually the biological mother. A "good mother" represents a home base, shelter from the storm, physical and emotional security, nurturance; she is the figure we cling to or run to when distressed. Suppose, instead, that this same figure is the source of our distress. When the adults do not provide a safe, nurturing environment, children must find a way to adapt. They think the adults are always right, so it must be me. This experience happens over and over and over, till it becomes internalized. The feeling of being inherently or hopelessly bad, or never good enough, is an attack on our true natures, our preciousness.

We react with defense mechanisms to survive in that environment. They revolve around the four main ways people defend themselves when they feel threatened: fight, flight, freeze, or placate and appease (fawn). Bill's strategy was the fight response; mine is more the placate and appease/codependency response. But we've probably all used all of them at various times. For more information on this topic, I recommend the book *Complex PTSD: From Surviving to Thriving*.[34] Complex PTSD (CPTSD) is caused by small traumas that happen repeatedly over a long period of time, rather than a big event like combat, a natural disaster, or rape. It is more like the type of water torture that goes drip, drip, drip. Walker considers emotional abuse and neglect to be the most harmful. Kids who were never hit may have no idea they were abused at all.

There have been many studies lately about the effects of microaggressions on people's mental and physical health.[35] "Microaggressions are the everyday slights, indignities, put-downs, and insults that members of marginalized groups experience in their day-to-day interactions with individuals who are often unaware that they have engaged in an offensive or demeaning way."[36] The author likens it to "death by a thousand cuts." I don't mean to detract attention from the marginalized groups in these studies, but who is more marginalized and powerless than children? In my story, I told about specific incidents I remembered, but how many others were there? How many times was I looked down on with contempt or made the butt of one of my father's jokes? These were not out-of-character behaviors for my parents; they were normal.

We have been conditioned to react in ways that allow us to survive but not thrive. This conditioning operates below our conscious awareness, like the fish that doesn't see any water. Like trauma survivors, we may have emotional flashbacks. Shame triggers, or people "pushing our buttons," send us into them. We may lash out at the other person, trying to ward off the feeling. When it comes, we are no longer present, we are six years old staring at the floor, face warm and flushed (or whatever your memory is), and can't hear what's being said. I was in a bad bicycle accident recently but didn't hit my head. The paramedic asked if I was wearing a helmet, and when I said no, he flashed me a look of contempt and disgust (to which I am highly sensitive and may have overinterpreted). I immediately felt contemptible and disgusting, even though a helmet was irrelevant to the accident. It was the way my mother often looked at me, and I cowered. I assumed no one at the hospital would want to take care of me. I cried because I felt so alone. It took me days—and friends—to get rid of that feeling. But it happens a whole lot less than it used to, and I don't stay in it for as long. I was just particularly vulnerable right then.

Remember, low self-esteem comes in different degrees and flavors. I'm not saying we all have CPTSD or that we're all shame-based at our core. Going through life feeling like we're not enough or not who we're supposed to be, or even that just one thing about us is horribly wrong, can be enough for us to be drawn to alcohol to numb our feelings.

Some parents are chronic worriers or always see the downside of things or expect the worst. Children pick up these habits, too. Many of us suffer more from anxiety than depression because these attitudes got wired in our brains. We don't feel safe or hopeful, which is unbearable.

Part of the reason alcoholism runs in families is that the same pattern keeps getting passed down the line—hurt children become parents who are emotionally immature and unintentionally hurt their children (because they don't know any better), who become parents, and so on down the line. Physical and sexual abuse are more easily brought into the light because we usually know when they are happening. We may not know we're being abused, but we do know something took place (unless the memories are repressed). Emotional and spiritual abuse are harder to acknowledge and easier to deny. *If we're not being hit or molested and there's food on the table, we think we have it good.* That's what I thought, yet I have vivid memories of all the shaming experiences I told in my story because I carried them around for decades after they happened.

Neglect is even harder to spot. It means looking for what *wasn't* there that should have been, but we don't know what that is. If you don't know if you were abused or neglected, check out *The Emotionally Absent Mother* (Cori, 2010); *Adult Children: The Secrets of Dysfunctional Families* (Friel & Friel, 2010); or *Adult Children of Emotionally Immature Parents: How to Heal from Distant, Rejecting, or Self-Involved Parents* (Gibson, 2015). You may think, why should I dig up stuff and create a new problem? Well, it's not a new problem. You have likely adapted to living without your basic human needs being met, either by denying them or finding dysfunctional ways to meet them, because you were forced to. We need to learn adult ways to handle our problems.

To recap on feelings—all feelings are okay, we can learn how to express them appropriately, and we're not responsible for other people's feelings. When I was not long out of treatment, I witnessed something that has made an impression on me to this day. I was dropping my son off at daycare, where he would only be for one hour before kindergarten. The director of the daycare was comforting a toddler who was crying because his mother was leaving. She was holding him and rubbing his back. And she said to him, "Don't cry. You've got nothing to cry about. You'll make your mother feel bad." She was actually saying, "Stuff your feelings. They're not valid. You're responsible for your mother's feelings. If she feels bad, it's your fault." This woman was not a bad person trying to damage a child, quite the opposite. And I'm sure it didn't feel like abuse to the child because he was being held and cuddled. But the message was shame-inducing and codependency-training-in-action. It should have been something like:

- You're sad and scared because your mom is leaving. *(Teach how to name the feeling.)*
- I understand you feel upset about that. *(Let the child feel heard, validate his experience.)*
- You don't want her to leave. *(Show understanding.)*
- She will come back for you, I promise. *(Reassure.)*
- I can hold you or you can go sit until you're ready to join the class. *(Offer solutions.)*

Granted, this woman was not the child's parent, but it's a great example of abuse not intended and not feeling like abuse.[37]

Basic Childhood Needs

Some of us may not remember or be able to see anything askew in our childhoods. But we may remember how we felt. Another way of getting at what we internalized as children is to look at the following list of basic human needs and see if they were being met. Maslow presented these as a hierarchy, with the most basic needs at the bottom, but for our purposes, we will just look at the list of basic human needs.[38] Here, I will only include examples that apply to children.[39]

1. **Physiological needs:** the bare minimum requirements for human survival—air, food, drink, shelter, clothing, warmth, sleep.
2. **Safety and security needs:** economic security, emotional security, social and familial stability, safety from physical attack and crime, a general feeling that the environment is safe and people follow the same rules (there's some predictability). Not living in fear.

3. **Love and belongingness needs**: the feeling of belonging in a family and community, loving and being loved, friendships, connectedness, feeling a part of, not outside looking in.

4. **Esteem needs**: two categories: (1) self-esteem, self-respect, self-confidence, achievement; and (2) social status—the respect of others in the community, good reputation.

Look at the list and walk yourself back in time. How did you feel when you were preschool age? When you went off to kindergarten? Elementary school? Middle school? High school? When you started drinking?

Did you feel safe, secure, loved, worthy, valued, and like you belonged? If you didn't feel that way as a child, there was something missing that you needed and it affected your development.

Gabor Maté, a Canadian physician who works with addicts, put forth the idea that we replace the word "addict" with "person in so much pain that this is the only way they can deal with it."[40] (Imagine what that would do to criminal justice and mental health systems!) For the people who are relating to this book, I think we could say "person in so much pain/shame/fear that drinking was the only way to cope." Children who do not grow up with their basic human needs met will continue to suffer as adults. It manifests in many different forms, one of which is alcoholism.

Still another way to access this information is by looking at our list of "shoulds." List all the things you think you're supposed to be or live up to (e.g., because you're a man, because you're a (last name), because you're a mother, etc.). Are you supposed to be happy all the time? Are you allowed to have problems or make mistakes? Are you man enough? Where did these ideas come from? Who put these pressures on you? Was it society, culture, or ourselves? Is it who *you* want to be? This pressure to be something we're not, or not enough, is a message that who we actually are is not okay. We have not experienced unconditional love. We may be loved, but we are loved more when we act in certain ways. We learned to distort ourselves in order to get that love. We are separated from our true selves, and it damages our spirit. It takes away our preciousness.

It's not essential to have the exact facts about what happened to us. If we can recognize that for whatever reason, we did not develop normally, that's enough. We will see how the survival skills we learned in childhood did their job because we survived. But now we need some better tools.

We are going to use the AA program to stay sober and recover the preciousness we were born with. Part of being restored to sanity is acknowledging that we are just as good as anyone else. "It is our birthright to know ourselves as glorious, innocent creations." (Larsen & Hegarty, 1987)[41] Try to sit with that for a moment. Does it feel uncomfortable? Do you remember ever feeling that way? When did it go away?

"Knowing we are adequate and worthy is fundamental to sane living."[42] With the possible exception of lemmings, organisms do not normally cause harm to themselves. People who treat themselves badly are out of sync with the very nature of life on earth. Self-preservation is sane. Self-destruction, self-sabotage, and self-deprivation are not. Our goal is sober and sane living, so we will have to take a look at these traits.

6

FEELINGS

The *Big Book* does not talk much about feelings, except for fear and anger. It tells us to ask God to remove these feelings. People like to point out, "There's no chapter called Into Feeling." Or they say feelings aren't facts and dismiss them. It is a fact that our feelings influence our thoughts and behavior, consciously or unconsciously. Ignoring them does not make them go away, nor does it stop them from seeking an outlet.

> *Feelings are like children—we don't have to let them drive the car, but we cannot just keep locking them in the trunk.*

That's the very definition of emotional baggage. In my opinion, AA short-circuits the emotional healing process. "God, save me from being angry" is asking God to help me repress my feelings. Why not, "God, help me work through this feeling?" Because they don't really go away until we work through them.

It has been said that alcoholics are emotionally immature. That was true for me. I was taught not to listen to anything below the neck. We were learning the whole time, just like other kids. But we were learning different things: how to hide our feelings, how to be manipulative when we couldn't ask directly, how to be passive-aggressive when anger wasn't tolerated, and how to keep people away from us with sarcasm or an unfriendly demeanor so they wouldn't see our broken insides or because we were afraid. So, we *are* delayed in learning more functional ways to handle emotions. For more information on emotions, I recommend *Emotional Intelligence* by Daniel Goleman[43] and the previously mentioned Gibson book, *Adult Children of Emotionally Immature Parents.*

Having feelings is a normal part of being human. We have them because they serve the evolutionary purpose of survival. They aren't good or bad; they just are. Feelings give us information about ourselves, information I was taught to ignore for so long, I was barely aware of it. Fight (anger) or flight (fear) are basic responses to a perceived threat, to keep us safe. Anger gives us immediate power and strength to defend ourselves. Fear/flight says, "Run away, you can't win." Feeling pain, hurt, or sadness tells us what is important to us—if we didn't care, it wouldn't hurt; it also brings healing and connection with others, as it is part of the human condition. Guilt tells us we have done something wrong (which may be fixable). Joy, happiness, and other positive emotions are good for our health and make life worth living. Loneliness signifies our need for connection—we evolved in social groups, not as loners. Loners didn't survive. Emotions are part of the long history of human evolution, and we are not allowing ourselves the full extent of our humanity when we refuse to acknowledge them.

Healthy shame tells us we're not God; we can't just do whatever we want all the time. Its evolutionary purpose is to inhibit or hide any behavior that might get us kicked out of our social group since our survival depends on being in the group. A person should have enough shame to keep them from going grocery shopping naked.

Toxic shame tells us we are bad in our very being (not redeemable). We have been rejected. Bill W. could only see himself as being at the top of the heap or underneath it. I saw myself more as outside of it (kicked out of the group, or sure I would be if they only knew me).

Humans are hard-wired to be on the lookout for danger. It's easy to see why natural selection would favor this. We are also hard-wired to hang on to negative experiences so we can try to avoid the same trouble next time. But there are no dangerous animals or warring bands trying to kill us anymore. The danger that I was always on the lookout for was getting my feelings hurt, being laughed at, or being exposed as an impostor. We might call it being on the lookout for social dangers. This same group I was born into, that I needed in order to survive, was itself a threat.

People with toxic shame see social danger everywhere. I was always worried about what other people think, fearing their disapproval. In AA, I learned that no one was actually paying that much attention to me, and these fears were more fancied than real. The way I was told this, however, was kind of hurtful. They said, "You're not that special; you're not that important." To accuse me of thinking I'm special or important was a shame trigger. I didn't feel special or important; I felt like my defects were glaring and people couldn't help but notice. AA taught me that this was part of my self-centeredness as an alcoholic, that I was bad for doing it. I later learned that the habit of thinking people notice us more than they actually do is a cognitive bias called the spotlight effect, prevalent in egocentric cultures such as ours, and is pretty normal.[44] The abnormal part was my certainty of their disapproval (shame). I realize the AA people had good intentions, but you don't heal shame by telling someone they're bad.

Alcohol numbs our feelings. Unfortunately, it is not selective and numbs *all* our feelings. Many people become alcoholics because being in an altered state of mind is more comfortable than being in their natural state of mind. My drinking was a deliberate attempt to overcome my crippling self-consciousness, numb my feelings, and quiet my negative self-talk. So, while alcohol for a long time seems like the solution, not the problem, it is not sustainable physically or emotionally. All the feelings we don't deal with aren't gone. They're locked in the trunk, which is about to explode, and they leak out sideways affecting our relationships.

Parents are supposed to help their kids identify their feelings and work out strategies for handling them.[45] Often, they just need to feel validated, to have their reality mirrored back, as in, "I see you're frustrated," or "You seem sad. What's going on?" That is not what I got from my parents. My emotions were bad or wrong (civilized people don't get angry), invalidated (you don't really feel that way), or to be ignored while I put on a good act demonstrating the socially appropriate feelings I should be having. I did not know how to recognize or name many of my emotions. I was never angry at people who were close to me (it's not safe, bad things happen when people get angry; also, if you're angry at your spouse, it means you don't love him). I didn't even have names for how I was feeling—good or bad, that was it.

I got terrible headaches for which there was no medical cause. A therapist taught me how to recognize the physical manifestations of anger: hot head, energy rising, the feeling you're about to blow. These lasted in me only for a second before I shut them down and got a headache. Once I started saying I'm angry, or even yelling it in my car or an empty restroom, I felt a tremendous relief and no headache. Sometimes anger sneaks up on me. I catch myself swearing or being easily frustrated, and I have to take a step back and go, wait—this probably means I'm angry about something! What is it? When you come into AA, they say HALT—hungry, angry, lonely, tired. I also had no idea if or when I was lonely. For me, feeling unconnected was normal. I didn't have a name for it.

Culture also affects how we deal with feelings. In our culture, it's okay for men to get angry, but they're not supposed to cry. For women, it's okay to cry but not to get angry. Some men, when they feel sad or hurt, show anger instead because it's more acceptable. How many bar fights have been started over hurt feelings? Some women convert anger into emotional pain for the same reason—"I'm not mad; I'm just hurt." As a broad generalization, I'd say that men are more likely to develop Bill's personality type because it embodies the John Wayne stereotype they were fed, while very few women grow up believing they are omnipotent and still have to fight for equality. These are just examples; it varies by culture.

We have been locking feelings in the trunk for quite some time now. They are still there, clamoring to be let out. If we don't deal with them directly, they will deal with us indirectly. We may cry a lot at movies because we have stored up pain we can't face in real life. We may rage because of all our repressed anger, and it will come out at the wrong person or out of proportion to the incident. Grief and depression may show in our body language and lack of self-care. We will work through a lot of this emotional baggage when we do the Steps. But we need instructions.

Emotional maturity is a process. It takes time. And it takes processing one episode or event at a time. Here's a basic procedure that has worked well for me:

1. I notice that I'm feeling something. It's usually an energy that makes me want to move toward or away from something.

2. I put a name to the feeling and own it. This is my reaction to this situation. I'm entitled to any reaction whatsoever. I am not acting on it, I'm just having it.

3. I say out loud if possible, or at least to myself:

   - I'm angry! I am so pissed right now!

- I'm scared. I don't know what's going to happen, and I'm afraid.
- I am really hurting. Something I care about is slipping away, and it hurts!
- I am so sad right now. I feel a big loss inside of me.

These are a few examples. Just own the feeling instead of repressing it. Don't judge it. Don't take it out on someone else. It's not right or wrong; we are organisms having a reaction to a stimulus. The reaction we have depends on our nature and our previous experience and conditioning. This is good information for me to have about myself. It's frequently how my prior conditioning is revealed to me. Remember, emotions are there to help us respond to threats quickly, bypassing the rational thought process and telling us to act immediately. However, our lives are rarely threatened today. We can take our time to parse the situation and decide how we want to respond.

AA literature tells us to pause when agitated and practice restraint of tongue and pen. Good advice, but then what? It doesn't always go away that fast. I continue to vent and/or talk about the feeling with someone else or sleep on it until the emotional energy is discharged or significantly lessened. It will happen. It may take a lot of crying, a long cooling-off period, or a lot of reassurance, but it will happen. This too shall pass. Sometimes I picture a toddler banging on her highchair. She tires out eventually. Maturation is a process. We don't make the best decisions based on emotion. If there's not enough time to go through this procedure, I at least do the pause, breathe, and recognize the feeling and how it may cloud my judgment. It's okay to ask for more time to respond.

Now I am in a much better space to decide if or how I want to respond to the situation. I can go through a rational and principled decision-making process. Decisions often involve value judgments. Choosing a response that fits with my value system shows integrity and boosts my self-esteem.

Here's my favorite example of owning our feelings instead of pushing them onto someone else (which was probably done to us repeatedly). My friend didn't like what her husband was wearing. She did not say, "You're wearing that?" That implies he's the problem. She said, "I don't have enough self-esteem for you to leave the house dressed like that." I frequently wanted to (or did) punish someone who "made me feel bad about myself." Now I own the fact that the shame that was triggered was already inside of me. They didn't put it there. And how I feel about myself is up to me.

In my experience, many of the things the program asks us to do—accept, forgive, let go—are not things I can just do because I'm "supposed" to. I spent way too much time telling myself I'm bad, I'm not working a good program, I should be able to do this by now, what's wrong with me—all because I couldn't do these things on command. I learned that I get to the desired end state by going through the process I just described—allowing myself to have all the feelings that arise, honoring them, and moving on, somewhat like the stages of grieving. Acceptance is the last stage, not the first. Forgiveness comes after I stand up to the person in my head, tell them I'm pissed and I did not deserve to be treated that way, and eventually come to accept that they are flawed, as am I, and I'd rather put it behind me and get along. I may have to do it more than once over the same incident. Bill tells us we cannot afford to be angry, but that's not exactly correct. As humans, we cannot help but become angry. As alcoholics, we cannot afford to hang onto the anger and have it turn into a resentment. The process above helps work through and release the anger so this doesn't happen.

Many people, either now or in the past, tell us how we're "sup-posed" to feel about certain things. For example, I should be happy for a co-worker who gets promoted over me. But I cannot command myself to feel that way. In the long run, I would like to have a peaceful relation-ship with my co-worker, but right now, I'm angry and jealous and feel I was treated unfairly. And in my old programming, I'm also bad because I'm supposed to feel happy for her. I have to let go of the "shoulds" and "supposed-tos" and start with how I actually feel right now. In a couple days, I may be ready to go to the supervisor and say, "I was really hoping to get that promotion. Obviously, you felt she deserved it and I did not. I'm not questioning your judgment, but could you please give me any feedback on what I need to improve to merit a position like that?"

Everyone carries around with them in their mind some sort of working model below their conscious awareness about how the world functions—who am I, what are people like, am I safe, do I belong, etc. When something doesn't match our model, we adjust the model to match reality. If we mature in a healthy fashion, the model becomes less black and white, more complex, more nuanced. But if we felt threatened as children, we developed defense mechanisms—variations of fight, flight, freeze, and appease. They helped us to not get hurt, but they also prevented us from maturing. Instead of having an open, exploring atti-tude toward new experiences, our focus was on staying safe.

Most people broaden their horizons as they grow up. Their world gets bigger. They see new things that don't fit previous conceptions and grow into broader perspectives. But we have been shut down, full of defense mechanisms, living in fear—whether we were aware of it or not. When we did that, we shut the door on our emotional growth. We were on lock-down. We are still living with the model we acquired at a very young age. We don't see things as they are; we see things as we are.

When our working model doesn't grow and change to better fit the current reality, we suffer. It's almost like we're still trying to master checkers while everyone else has moved on to playing chess.

Most educated people understand the difference between anecdotal evidence and actual data. A new medication is tried out on many people before it gets FDA approval. They can't give it to one or two people who have no side effects and then claim it's safe for everyone. It's the same with us and our world-view and conditioned responses. I assume *everyone* out there is dangerous—they want to see me make a fool of myself, tell me I'm fat, or don't want me around—based on my own anecdotal experiences of growing up in my particular family. The rest of the world is not thinking any of those things or even thinking about me at all. That's me viewing the world through my past experience. It doesn't match reality. To mature emotionally means to open up little by little and recognize that we have extrapolated way too broadly based on our unique anecdotal experiences. Open-mindedness is essential to recovery.

When my mental model causes panic, I need someone to talk me off the ledge. Now I can do it for myself a lot of times, but at first, it required help. When I only have one way of seeing things, I need to be shown other ways. One time, I was going to a meeting in a new place, in a split-level building with stairs going up and stairs going down. There was an AA sign between them. I completely froze in my tracks and held my breath. Why? I was afraid I was about to look stupid and would be made fun of and ridiculed if I made the wrong move. That's my conditioned response. Then I paused and thought, well, if I do choose the wrong stairs, it's probably happened before and is no big deal. Plus, it's 6:45 a.m., so there's probably not even anyone here except for those attending the meeting. I happened to choose the correct stairway, and everything was fine.

Another time, a judge was trying to humiliate me in open court. I immediately started to go into shame—my conditioned response. Then I stopped and thought, Why should I feel humiliated? He's the one who's acting immaturely, and the rest of the courtroom can see that. I'll just stand here and wait till he's done. The quicker I can catch myself going into shame or some other oversized reaction, the better the outcome. Once it's there in full force, I lose the ability to think. Trauma reactions circumvent the rational part of the brain. We are like Pavlov's dogs trying not to salivate; we've been conditioned to react in certain ways, and now we're trying to break that conditioning.

In some situations, no matter how hard we try, we may still feel ongoing anger. This is usually because the provoking stimulus is still present. It happens to me in traditional AA meetings, where the reading of "How It Works," if I pay close attention, invalidates my entire sobriety. I've learned to tune it out.

In early sobriety, our emotions are all over the place because we're off our meds (alcohol). We have stronger reactions than the situation warrants because we haven't been feeling anything for so long. We direct our anger at the wrong people simply because they're available and safe. We mourn the loss of our best friend (alcohol). We're fidgety—restless, irritable, and discontent—because we don't know what to do with ourselves. We're lonely for our drinking friends. We're afraid we're going to relapse or never have fun again. Most of these we can just let pass, recognizing that we're coming off alcohol and this is normal. We can practice noticing and owning what we're feeling. Just naming it out loud and/or sharing about it in a meeting provides a great deal of relief. Then we can just let it go.

There's not a deep-seated underlying cause for everything we feel. Feelings (and thoughts) are like pop-up windows—we can choose to pay attention or we can say, "Isn't that curious," and just hit escape. It's the ones that show a pattern or cause us repeated trouble that deserve the most attention.

Emotions are our informants. They show us how we've been conditioned. They are the entry point into working on recovery.

One cautionary word about feelings—know when to stop. Besides our gut emotional reactions, we can also think ourselves into feelings. We can create anxiety by getting into the "what ifs." We can create pain, self-pity, and shame by getting into the "if onlys." We can fuel our anger by dredging up a list of other things we're mad at this person about that we haven't dealt with yet. If we get into these, we can set a timer for fifteen minutes and then take a walk or call a friend. We do not want to get stuck in such fruitless pursuits that don't lead anywhere good.

7
STEP ZERO

We improved our self-esteem and attitude enough to begin working
the Twelve Steps.

Negative Self-Talk

I was pretty beat down when I arrived in AA. Being an alcoholic was just one more nail in the coffin of being a defective loser. Working the Steps, to me, looked like submitting myself to the beating I deserved for being an alcoholic. I didn't see anything positive about it. In hindsight, I wish that someone had told me, "Let's work on your self-esteem first, to get it up to a point where you can contemplate taking a look at yourself without it feeling like a punishment and possibly even see it as an opportunity." Nearly every thought or feeling I had about myself was negative. Assuming you feel the same way, we have to get up to sea level before we can start climbing the steps. (For me, this included anti-depressants, too.)

We are going to work the Steps to stay sober and improve our self-esteem. We are creating something—a healthier, happier person and a more fulfilling life. It is not a punishment—it's a tremendous opportunity.

Our self-talk is such a habit, we don't even notice it. Or we don't think it's negative, we think it's deserved. Or, it's the only way we know how to motivate ourselves—because we will be so terrible if we don't do this. If building self-esteem is like knitting a sweater, then negative self-talk is the yarn we pull on to unravel the whole thing. It is counterproductive, to say the least, to be stitching something together with one hand and pulling it apart with the other. Or, to use a different analogy, we are trying to build our secure home base within us. We can't build up our insides to feel at home with ourselves while the termites of self-criticism keep eating it away.

It is nearly impossible to completely rid ourselves of self-criticism because we have been doing it forever. It's almost like deciding to change your dominant hand. You could probably do it, but it would take a lot of time, attention, and conscious effort. No one can maintain that degree of conscious effort all the time. We would expect on many occasions to use the old hand and not even notice. With practice, we might catch ourselves sometimes—Oops! Used the wrong hand. Think of this the same way. It is that hard. Going on autopilot, doing it the old way, will happen a lot. We will not beat ourselves up over that. It's completely expected. It's how brain wiring works.

I once jokingly said that neuroplasticity is my Higher Power because that is truly where my hope lies. One of the reasons recovery requires a sustained effort is because without the continued effort to stay on the new path, we will end up back on the old one. Neuroplasticity works both ways. If we stop using the new connections, they will weaken, and the old ones are still there. Malcolm Gladwell put forth the hypothesis that to truly master a skill takes 10,000 hours.[46] That's hours of actually practicing the instrument or playing the sport. Let's say we spend three hours a day being consciously aware of our new recovery mindset. By his estimate, it will take nine years before we start to default to our new way of thinking instead of the old way. So please, be gentle and patient with yourselves.

I thought I had two good reasons for being hard on myself. One was for motivation, but I learned in recovery that positive motivation works much better. We are not going to work the Steps because we are bad and full of character defects. We are going to work the Steps to recognize what is right in us, work on the things that get in the way of living our lives fully, and build something beautiful: a person who knows who s/he is; likes that person; feels secure enough to be authentic and vulnerable; and lives with integrity but not perfectly, and that's okay.

The second reason was more sinister. I believe I developed it as a defense mechanism to avoid being blindsided by criticism. If I'm already thinking worse of myself than anyone else could, then what they say won't hurt so much. It won't be as bad as what I'm already saying about myself. Can you imagine if we were talking about physical rather than emotional pain? I cut myself up all the time so if someone else tries to cut me, it won't be such a big deal? I already have self-inflicted scars all over my body, so you can't scar me. That's crazy. It's just as crazy to do what I was doing.

One of the things I did to work on my self-talk was to use affirmations. Get out two pieces of paper. On the first one, write down all the negative things you frequently say to yourself. On the other, write a positive statement that's the opposite of each one. You can make it aspirational (not true yet) or something you can actually believe.

For example:

Negative Statement	Aspirational Statement	Believable Statement
Nobody likes me.	Everybody likes me.	Many people like me.
I'm a mistake since birth.	I'm a glorious innocent creation.	I have just as much right to be here as anyone else.
I screwed up again.	I see mistakes as opportunities.	Everybody makes mistakes.
I'm fat and unlovable.	I am totally lovable, no matter what.	I'm not fat; I just have a fat body image, and I'm lovabie whether I'm fat or not.
I'm a bad mother.	I'm a fabulous mother.	I'm a good enough mother, and that's all that's expected of anyone.
I'm lazy, selfish, and irresponsible	I excel in effort, empathy, and conscientiousness.	I care about others and do my best.
I'm such a loser; I burden people with my presence.	Everyone loves and respects me and is glad I'm here.	I'm not that different from everyone else; we're all unique and we all belong.
Everyone thinks they're better than me, and they're right.	Everyone adores me just the way I am.	No one is judging me all the time. Only I do that, and I can stop it.
I'm not good enough, smart enough, witty enough, or thin enough.	I am more than enough in everything about me.	I am enough. Period. Everyone has room for improvement.

I can't do any-thing right.	I do everything right.	I am competent enough and do most things right most of the time.
I'll never amount to anything.	I'm already a success, and I keep getting better every day.	I am coming into my own at my own pace, and it's perfect for me.
I'm such an asshole. I can't believe anyone puts up with me.	I love myself all the time, no matter what.	When I'm down on myself, I treat myself with compassion the same way I would a troubled friend.

Table 2. Affirmations

I like the aspirational statements because they offset the equally untrue negative things we've been telling ourselves. It's a deliberate swing of the pendulum too far to the other side so that we can end up in the middle. But some people feel silly saying those, and you don't have to. If you cannot come up with a positive believable statement, ask a close friend or loved one. They will be able to tell you good things about yourself easily.

Tell the negative statements, "Thank you for protecting me the best way you knew how. Through no fault of your own, it turns out your efforts were misguided. I have better ways to protect myself now. I hope you enjoy your retirement. I'm sure I'll see you around."

If you can't come up with anything, here are some generic examples that may appeal to you:

- I am a worthwhile person, deserving of love.
- I honor all my feelings.
- I deserve the good things in life.

- I am safe today.
- I decide what my own values and standards are.
- I have a right to make mistakes just like everyone else. Making a mistake does not mean I am a mistake.
- I am a precious child of God, and God doesn't make junk.
- I let go of what other people may think of me. What matters most is what I think of me (or what God thinks of me).
- I treat myself with compassion, the same way I would treat a friend.
- I am wholly adequate to handle any situation because I can always ask for help.
- I delight in my humanity and all that comes with it.

Read the affirmations out loud and make a recording of it. For me, saying nice things to myself was like breaking a taboo because in my house, the first commandment was "Thou shalt not approve of thyself!" The key to rewiring the brain is repetition. Listen to the recording several times a day, several days a week, for several months. You're trying to replace the old recordings in your head with new ones. Feel free to make changes and additions as you recognize the need. Instead of recording, you can also read these out loud several times a day. You just have to hear yourself saying them.

If that's too much, try to look at yourself in the mirror every morning and say something positive. "Hi, Beth. I'm happy to see you today." So many days I did not feel that way, but I said it anyway. All these things feel silly, but they work if we keep at them.

Another tool I continue to use when the negative talk is about a certain situation is this: Try to describe the situation as objectively as you can and then pretend it is not you but a friend who is going through this experience. I am so much nicer to others than I am to myself. Now we are learning to be a friend to ourselves, so say the same thing to yourself.

What I Say to Myself	What I'd Say to a Friend
You brought this on yourself. You deserve it.	Sounds like you're going through a really tough time. Take it easy on yourself.
You suck. You can't handle anything. Why do you bother to get up in the morning?	It's not your fault. There are many factors beyond your control.
I came in second. LOSER! What a wasted effort.	That's fantastic! Congratulations. All your hard work paid off.
Everyone is staring at you because of your glaring imperfections. You shouldn't go out in public.	You look fine. No one pays any attention to the little things we focus on about ourselves.
I lost my job—I'm unemployable. Don't let anyone know.	Another job will come along, your friends and family will support you.

Table 3. Self vs. Friend

The golden rule for codependents ought to be, "Do unto yourself as well as you do unto others." We are well-practiced at seeing what other people need in terms of emotional support and giving it to them. It's time to turn that skill around and use it on ourselves, too. Don't we deserve to be treated like a friend? Which kind of treatment are we (or anyone) most likely to benefit from? *Kindness does more good than harsh judgment. Self-compassion yields better results than self-flagellation.*

Have you ever actually listened to the critical voices? Do some of them sound like a specific person's voice yelling at or criticizing you? For example, are you saying "I'm such a loser" or "you're such a loser"? The "you" voice is probably coming from someone else. Anytime I'm in the house on a nice day, my mom still yells at me, "You kids are so lazy! Why aren't you outside?" I've been doing an early morning Zoom meeting, where some of the participants are jogging, hiking, or bicycling during the meeting, and to me, it feels like a punch to the gut, accompanied by, "I'm bad because I'm not doing that." It's my Pavlovian response that happens before I have a chance to think about it. I have to talk that one down. "Mom, you probably just wanted us out of the house so you could have peace and quiet. I've outlived you by four years already and am in better shape than you were the last twenty years of your life. I think I can decide when and how I will exercise."

If some of your negative voices sound like other people's voices, take a look at that. Was that an appropriate thing to say to a child? People dumped their baggage on us, and now we can verbally give it back. "That's your issue, not mine." "When I had a fight with my friends, you should have said, 'What happened?' not 'I hate you.' That's really a no-brainer for a parent. You were the failure right then, not me." Or, "I'm an adult now and not dependent on you. If you keep talking to me that way, I will walk away." I'm talking back to the voice, not the actual person. If we don't stop these voices from repeating, shame is truly the gift that keeps on giving. We perpetuate the abuse by telling ourselves the same things we were told. This is why I say we can't build our self-esteem while working the Steps if we are simultaneously tearing it down.

If we are constantly giving ourselves "not enough" messages, let's look at that. I'm not (blank) enough. What do you put in the blank? Let's challenge that statement. Try to answer these questions: Enough for what? Enough for who? What would be enough? Define it. Is that a realistic standard? Is it realistic considering everything else you're doing? What are *your* priorities?

A lot of "not-enoughness" comes from having been loved more when we performed in accordance with someone else's standards. If only I were more (blank), I would get the love and attention I need. We internalized this belief because we had parents who were not capable of loving and valuing us unconditionally, which is what we deserved. Now we know that the way we were treated was not about us. It was about them. Aren't boundaries wonderful?

Negative Attitudes

I also had to change my habit of focusing on the negative. One time, before I was sober, I had to drive somewhere way across town with no freeways, and I remember telling someone indignantly when I got there, "I hit seventeen red lights!" They asked, "How many were green?" I had no idea. I just had the habit of focusing on the negative. *What we focus our attention on is a choice.* I probably would have been in a much better mood if I had counted the green lights. I have used several techniques to change this habit or to counteract it when I realize I am doing it. Now when I'm driving, I play the Facebook "Like" game. I look around and see how many things I can like—person walking a dog, person exercising, not much traffic, my tax dollars at work fixing roads, person wearing a colorful shirt, car with a funny bumper sticker, green light, etc. It actually uplifts my mood.

Another positivity exercise is the saying, "A thousand things are going to go right today." It's true. We take so many things for granted. I start listing them. I woke up sober; in my own bed; with a roof over my head; water came out of the faucet; hot water came out of the hot water faucet; I had clothes to wear to work; my car started (that's probably a thousand things right there that had to work right); I didn't get in an accident; I wasn't delayed by traffic, etc. When any one of these things goes wrong, we're shocked or furious. The whole world comes crashing down on us. But there is generally a whole lot more going right than there is going wrong. We just don't notice it. When you feel overwhelmed, stop and notice what's going right.

And of course, there's the AA favorite—the gratitude list. This gets us on the track of being grateful for what we have, rather than bemoaning what we don't have. It's not to deny that we have wants or needs, but it can help to keep them in perspective.

Another thing that helps to build self-esteem is to treat ourselves to things we normally would deny ourselves. These are things that many normal people do, but for us, it's hard:

- Take a bubble bath. *Oh, that's so self-indulgent.*
- Buy something for yourself. *No, the money is better spent on something else.*
- Relax. *No, I'm not comfortable when I'm not being productive.*
- Enjoy nature. *Well, I really should be working.*
- Try a hobby. *Oh, that's so frivolous.*
- Read a novel. *No, only nonfiction because life is serious.*
- Take time out for art, music, creativity. *No, these are foolish luxuries.*

What's something you think you'd enjoy that other people "get away with," but you won't allow yourself to do? Do it anyway. It will feel like a guilty pleasure, like you really shouldn't. But then you will see that nothing bad came of it, and next time, it will feel a little less uncomfortable. Take the action to create new neural pathways that allow you to live more fully. We are not becoming over-indulgent when we do these things. We are giving ourselves space to not be so driven, to let our guard down. As far as "live and let live" goes, we have been good at letting others live but not so good at living for ourselves. If other people deserve these things, then so do we.

One last ongoing exercise before starting the Steps. We are going to have to try out new behaviors that feel uncomfortable, but this one is totally safe and a good place to start. When someone pays you a compliment, say thank you. Period. Do not argue, deflect, minimize, or try to guess their motive. Take them at their word. Even allow for the possibility that their opinion of you is likely far more objective than yours. Try to let it actually sink in. The compliment may be well-deserved.

Some books that help deal with the inner critic are *Healing Your Emotional Self, Freedom from your Inner Critic,* and *Complex PTSD: From Surviving to Thriving.*[47]

Now that we are feeling a little better about ourselves, we will approach the Steps with a positive attitude. They look scary to everyone, but we are particularly sensitive to words like shortcomings, defects, morals. It looks like we are going to tear into ourselves and admit all our horrible failings. But it's not like that. We are on a journey of self-discovery. We are likely going to find out that we're not half as bad as we thought we were. We will see that we have some habits or tendencies that block us from becoming happy, sane, sober people. We want and deserve the good life for ourselves. We will be glad to learn what has been tripping us up, so we don't fall into the same holes again—holes of shame, anxiety, depression, and alcohol. There's a prize at the end! A new, sober you with a solid sense of self and of belonging in a community.

8

STEP ONE

We admitted that we were powerless over alcohol—that our lives had become unmanageable.[48]

In Step One, we admit to being powerless over alcohol and having trouble managing our lives. The *Big Book* does a good job of driving home the point about powerlessness over alcohol. Sobriety is the *sine qua non* of the rest of this work, so by all means delve thoroughly into your relationship with alcohol and the consequences.

In the *Twelve & Twelve*, the alcoholic personality is mentioned: self-centered in the extreme, no humility, refuse to admit defeat, "what's in it for me" attitude. That does not describe us. For me, admitting powerlessness was *yet another* thing wrong with me, and I didn't know if I could bear it. I balked at being labeled an alcoholic because it was an actual confirmation that I was bad. I was still looking good on the outside, and now everyone would know it had all been a lie. "What's in it for me" was not my first, second, or even third thought when it came to decision making. I felt undeserving, not entitled. But if it would help someone else, I'd be all over it—codependent. Doing something good for myself was foreign. I used to motivate myself to lose weight because my kids didn't deserve a fat mother, not because I wanted to be healthy. *Getting sober is something we do for ourselves because we want a better life. No matter how we get here, we are unlikely to stay unless we are internally motivated.*

I also admitted I was powerless over others—the first step in Codependents Anonymous. I had been living under the mistaken belief I could control what people think of me by showing them only what I wanted them to see. It's called impression management. Whenever people came over, my house had to look perfect, so no one could question my respectability. Then I heard a guy in a meeting say that whenever they left a party, his Al-Anon wife would comment, "I can't believe they don't polish their doorknobs!" I suddenly saw the futility in trying to control people's impressions. It's impossible to imagine everything anyone might pick up on.[49]

I was never the controlling type who thought she knew best and had advice for everyone—the actor's scenario in the *Big Book*. But I felt responsible for other people's feelings. I believed that people who have more than they deserve (like me) have to constantly give of themselves and try to make *other* people happy. In fact, *my* being happy is selfish—it shows that I'm not thinking about those less fortunate. Now I know I cannot control anyone else's feelings. Al-Anon quotes Abraham Lincoln: "Most folks are about as happy as they make up their minds to be." It's totally an inside job. We can't make anyone else happy. We can't make anyone love us. We *can* hitch our own wagon to our own star.

When it comes to unmanageability, we have to explore both our drinking and our low self-esteem. Sobriety comes first, so thoroughly explore all the ways that your drinking has affected your life and the lives of those around you, the same way everyone else works this step. You have to be sober to do the rest of this work.

Low self-esteem made our lives unmanageable long before we started drinking. Denying our true selves in order to survive has forced us to focus on how we're supposed to act, how we're supposed to feel, and what we're supposed to think, in order to appease and placate the big people. In other words, the way we *actually are* is wrong or bad. This is the message we internalized, and we learned how to be what other people want us to be. In a healthy family, we'd be learning about ourselves—our own feelings and how to manage them, our own desires and how to fulfill some of them, our own thoughts and how to make sense of things. *Living in a grown-up world without grown-up skills is unmanageable.* Being out of touch with our true selves is a hollow feeling—right inside me where the "me" is supposed to be, there's nothing but an abandoned child, and no one remembers her name anymore. We are so filled with angst that it's like air to us; we don't even notice it. But all the same, it produces stress hormones, interferes with our immune systems, makes us feel restless, irritable, and discontent. Alcohol seemed to be the magic potion that took all this away. But now that alcohol is not an option, we realize the true solution is to do this work so that we can be comfortable in our own skin. Many of us arrive in AA looking pretty good on the outside because that was our priority, but we are a mess on the inside. We knew we didn't really deserve the validation we got from others. We felt like impostors. We compartmentalized our lives and our thoughts to avoid cognitive dissonance. The unmanageability was internal.

At this point, we have admitted to being powerless over alcohol and others. These are both empirical facts. We can't control our drinking, and we can't control others. We have likely proven these to ourselves numerous times. But let's also look at what power we *do* have. We have a lot of power that we have not been using because we have been too afraid to stand up for ourselves or didn't know that was allowed or possible. A lot of us have lived our lives seeking validation and approval from others, effectively giving them the power to determine how we feel about ourselves.

- We have the power to define ourselves and not be defined by others.
- We have the power to claim our worth and not let others determine it for us.
- We have the power to not take responsibility or blame for things out of our control or for someone else's bad behavior.
- We have the power to say no when we don't want to do something.
- We have the power to make our own decisions and accept the consequences.
- We have the power to define our roles in life according to our own standards.
- We have the power to let our voice be heard along with everyone else's.
- We have the power to walk away from bad situations.

I had to chuckle with the last one. I take a lot of group fitness classes, and sometimes, when there's a substitute instructor, people just up and leave ten to fifteen minutes into the workout. I decided if I ever wanted to do that, I would at least fake a limp when I walked out so as not to hurt her feelings. Still codependent!

So, Step One is actually very *empowering*. We're giving up the things we actually had no power over anyway, our drinking and other people; but we see that we have way more power in other areas than we may have realized. As a Step One exercise, continue the list I started. What power do you have? Read the list again, and replace the word "power" with "right." "I have the right to define myself and not be defined by others." Now read it again and replace the word "right" with "responsibility." "I have the responsibility to define myself and not be defined by others." This is how we claim ourselves as standalone people, not some unfortunate subset who didn't get the same things everyone else got.

9

STEP TWO

Came to believe that a power greater than ourselves could restore us to sanity.

In Step One, we admitted that our will power, although it may be great in some areas, failed at getting and keeping us sober. We needed help. To the nonalcoholic, alcohol is not cunning, baffling, or powerful. To us, it is because of our complicated relationship with it. It's that siren's call in our heads, speaking to us in our own voice, sounding perfectly reasonable to the unsuspecting. Every time I failed to make it as many days as I had planned without drinking, I just told myself I'd changed my mind. In reality, that was a rationalization after the fact. I gave in to the craving and tried to explain it away afterward. And I believed my explanation. This is one of the reasons I still go to meetings. Other people can easily see through my BS, but I frequently can't.

If you believe that your only help will come from a Higher Power that is loosely defined as all-powerful, in charge, loves you, and has a plan for your life, go with the *Big Book*. For me, I just needed help, and it came from many sources, the most important one being AA. There are many things I can't do by myself, like move a piano or fix my car. But I can get someone to help me or go to a place where someone has the necessary skills. I can consult a sponsor or put myself in the presence of people who are staying sober.

For us, restoration to sanity has two parts. First, there is the insanity of active alcoholism and all the thoughts, feelings, and behaviors that go along with it. During that part of our lives, we may actually have been like the alcoholic personality described in the book—selfish, self-centered, and stepping on toes. The need to drink overpowered our normally polite behavior. The *Big Book* covers this part of alcoholism.

But, were we really sane before we started drinking? Recall that knowing we are adequate and worthy is fundamental to sane living. "Restore" is really not the right word here if we have no memory of ever feeling good about ourselves. We have to learn it from scratch. I have a baby picture of myself smiling like, "Hello, world. I'm here and I feel good about it." I have no memory of it, but I've been working on restoring myself to that. I accept it as a fact that I am intrinsically good (not perfect or infallible), and all this recovery work can allow that little light to shine again. Most days it does, so I have faith that it works. I have seen it happen to other alcoholics, so I have hope and faith in the process.

The recovery work is learning how to feel and express my feelings, changing my perceptions of myself and others, letting go of self-limiting beliefs, trying new behaviors, allowing (or forcing) myself to take risks and be vulnerable, clearing away the wreckage of the past, and more. I cannot do these things by myself. How can you fix relationship problems without being in relationships? How can you begin to feel like you fit in without being around others? When I first read the Twelve Steps, I looked at them as an academic exercise (because I was unaware of the other parts of being a person). I wanted to rush through them as an achievement and get a year in six months. Turns out, they involve growing up emotionally and spiritually. It takes a year's growth to get a year. It takes being emotional and practicing the principles one day at a time.

Left to its own devices, my brain on autopilot repeats what I learned in childhood. I needed new input. There was nothing wrong with the way my brain worked, but as the saying goes, garbage in, garbage out. When a sow's ear goes in, a silk purse doesn't come out. I knew how to be responsible and self-sufficient, but I didn't know who I was or how to be emotional, social, and interdependent. AA meetings and AA people are a great place to try out new behavior, check whether a long-held assumption is actually true, see if people are really thinking what you think they're thinking. AA people mirrored myself back to me more accurately than my family did because they didn't have their own agendas with me. Find a group that will love you until you learn to love yourself. Learning to trust others and be vulnerable requires a safe environment. You will find that in meetings, hopefully. Keep trying different meetings until you find one that feels right for you.

I've also read tons of recovery and self-help books, got medical help for depression, and worked with a therapist on family of origin and trauma issues. Don't be afraid to seek help in any area you may need it. These areas are outside issues as far as AA goes, but they can absolutely affect the quality of your sobriety. The lesson of Step Two for me is I need help, it's available, and it works.

10

STEP THREE

Made a decision to turn our will and our lives over to the care of God as we understood him.

Step Three is about making a decision to give up trying to run our lives by ourselves and accept other guidance. One way to do it is outlined in the *Big Book*. As Dr. Tiebout said, this admission of personal failure and not being God was an essential shift in perspective that was therapeutic for narcissists. Many people with low self-esteem also find value in turning their life over to a Higher Power. After all, we've been submitting to many other powers (e.g., alcohol, significant others, our parents' voices in our heads); it's healthier to submit to a pure, loving one. The thought that God doesn't make junk can be the foundation of new-found self-esteem. So if this works for you, stick with the *Big Book*.

When I was in treatment, I relapsed on cigarettes because it was the only relief valve they allowed. I had quit smoking five years earlier when I found out I was pregnant. I was supposed to do my Third Step with the chaplain, and I told him I couldn't. I was smoking, and I knew that wasn't God's will, so I would be a hypocrite if I did it and kept smoking. He tried to tell me that God was gentler than that, and if I were just learning how to walk, he would let me use a crutch. I thought that was a cop-out. This is how hard I was on myself at that time. Also,

I was pretty sure that God would find me disgusting for living a comfortable middle-class life while others were suffering, and once I took this Step, I would have to leave my family and go help Mother Teresa.

What worked for me was to make a commitment to being in recovery. It's a good exercise to write out what being in recovery means to you. My conception of recovery would be something like this, in no particular order except that the first two must come first:

- Total abstinence from mood-altering substances, except caffeine or as prescribed.
- I can't do this by myself. I need other resources besides my own, and I need to be part of a recovery community.
- Do my best to feel and manage my emotions.
- Remain teachable and keep learning every day.
- Strive for authenticity—be true to myself rather than putting on acts or masks.
- Develop and exercise boundaries—what's my part and what's beyond my part, where I end and someone else begins, where I have power and where I don't have power.
- Focus my energy on the things I can change—my attitude, my thoughts, my actions, working through emotions.
- Allow myself to be vulnerable when it seems safe to do so. Develop relationships where it is safe.
- Get out of my comfort zone and try new things.
- Live with integrity—develop a solid sense of who I am and what I'm about, and behave accordingly.
- Pay close attention to how I am treating myself and others— love and support produce better results than judgment and condemnation.

- Continue daily self-monitoring for unacknowledged feelings, behaviors, and attitudes that may impede my recovery.
- Instead of comparing and judging, be more compassionate with myself and others.
- Share my recovery with others if they are interested.
- Progress, not perfection.
- Have fun!

You can write out your own list and commit to it. You can change or add to the list any time, except for the first two. After my brother went through treatment and my mother attended his family week, he started drinking again. My mother said, "That doesn't really matter as long as he's living by the Twelve Steps." She conveniently overlooked the first one. Don't be like my mother.

The Third Step prayer talks about the "bondage of self." I imagine when Bill wrote this, he wanted to be relieved of his persistent thoughts of "I, me, mine;" "what's in it for me" attitude; self-aggrandizement; feelings of superiority; preoccupation with grandiose images of his success; sense of entitlement; being on a power drive, and the like. These things prevented him from staying sober, enjoying life, having healthy relationships, and being useful to others. But we, too, have the bondage of self. You know the saying that someone is "a prisoner of his own device"? Let's look at how we have been holding ourselves back:

- Self-loathing
- Self-doubt
- Self-sabotage
- Self-criticism
- Self-judgment
- Self-blame
- Self-seeking (approval, validation, praise, or attention)

- Self-effacing or self-deprecating attitudes
- Self-consciousness
- Self-defeating behaviors

Don't these stand in the way of our enjoying life, having healthy relationships, and being useful to others in a non-codependent way? For example, when we judge ourselves so harshly, we frequently start to judge others, too. When we accept more than our fair share of the blame for something, don't we invite becoming a dumping ground for others who accept too little responsibility? When we doubt our own feelings, thoughts, and perceptions, we will accept someone else's reality as our own, even though it doesn't fit. When we are too inhibited to try something new, we remain stuck in our comfort zone, which somehow keeps getting smaller. When we are too concerned about what others may think, we're not focused on what we think and what's right for us.

We are self-centered like Bill, but not just like Bill. We are not trying to dominate those around us, stepping on other people's toes and not noticing the damage to them. We are trying to protect ourselves from getting hurt. *Our coping behaviors damage us more than others.* To be in recovery means to stand up in the light of day and be counted as a worthy human being, just like everyone else. Whether you ask God to relieve you of this bondage or work on it with your sponsor and recovery community, or both, is up to you.

11

STEP FOUR

Made a searching and fearless moral inventory.

Step Four is the key to seeing ourselves as we really are. My contribution is mainly reframing the way we approach it and including some additional areas to look at. Yes, we want to get rid of the things in ourselves that have been blocking us, holding us back from becoming the eight-cylinder people we actually are, instead of running on just four. But first, we have to get past the negative language. We got down to causes and conditions when we looked at our upbringings, even though AA does not take it to that level. But then there is all this talk of flaws, failures, defects, and self – self – self. As a newcomer, I found these words very triggering—scolding and shaming. Granted, I did not end up in AA because I was so successful. But I had been trying to adhere to what I had been taught, believing it was the right way to be. It was hardly self-will run riot.

I was speaking with a veteran one time who had fought in Iraq and had PTSD. He said, "When I walk down the street, it's not the same as when you walk down the street. You probably think, oh, there's a tree, there's a bird. I think, what's behind that tree? What's under that bush? Is that bird carrying anything?" When he was in Iraq, these fears were completely rational; they were survival skills, not character defects. But back home, they interfered with his ability to enjoy life. Before recovery, I was a lot like him—people are lying in wait to make me look stupid, to call me out as fat, to laugh at me when I don't even know what's funny. Since these things had actually happened to me, they were rational fears, and it made sense to be hyper-vigilant.

However, when I carried them out into the bigger world, which turned out to be different from my home environment, they interfered with my ability to enjoy life. These character traits helped me survive— they were not flaws or failures. I doubt we would call the veteran an extreme example of self-will run riot in Iraq, always thinking about his own safety. I say thank you to all these behaviors and beliefs that helped me survive my childhood. But, now I'm an adult in a different environment. It's time to learn new behaviors and beliefs that are more adaptive to the world I live in today. Today, I approach Step Four with this attitude.

When I was a newcomer, it felt like punishment for being bad, and that was not very helpful. Whether a behavior is "good" or "bad," "moral" or "immoral," may well depend on the situation. It's more beneficial to call it useful or not useful in the given context. My negativity and pessimism were good when we held engineering design reviews and I got to say, "That won't work." My skepticism was conducive to being a defense attorney because the state has to prove the case beyond a reasonable doubt. I could always find something to doubt.

Why is the inventory so one-sided, focusing on the negative, not the positive? Doesn't that make us feel even worse? It's fine to inventory the things we appreciate about ourselves to not feel so lopsided. But our good qualities are not causing us problems. In Step Four, we want to find out what has not been working in our lives and caused us to resort to alcohol as a coping mechanism. In keeping with our self-esteem work, we may be sixty percent satisfied with ourselves by now. Don't lose sight of that big picture, but Step Four is for working on the other forty percent.

Resentments—People Who Harmed Us

We likely have resentments against the people who mistreated us. Bill glosses over people who harmed us quickly: just realize they were sick, forgive them, and move on. That didn't work for me. Getting over this stuff is a process, and he attempts to short-circuit it. These feelings are still locked in the trunk, and they have to come out.

The first feeling I have, once I am not in denial about the abuse, is compassion for the child. If I saw another child being treated the way I was, I would call it abuse. I feel compassion for myself. *It's not self-pity.* Sometimes there's a grief phase. "I'm so sorry that happened to you." There is usually anger, and it has probably been simmering for a long time.

One way of getting rid of this recurring anger is to allow ourselves to express it directly now, as adults, when we could not as children. The program tells us to keep our side of the street clean. That includes cleaning up the crap other people have left on it. For every slight or harm I told about in my story, I have gone back to each situation and stood up to the person who was abusive or not present. I have yelled at them:

- I am a dumbbell? You forced a gifted child to say she was stupid. That's a terrible way to treat a five-year-old! I'm glad she doesn't live with you anymore.
- I'm lazy, selfish, and irresponsible? No! You were. You didn't want to be bothered with any parental duties, so you made us do them. We were kids. We needed to have parents, not be parents.

- You glared at me with contempt and disgust when I wasn't even doing anything. Those feelings came from inside of you. I didn't provoke them. You didn't love me because you lacked the ability, not because I was undeserving.

- You shamed me for being born into your socioeconomic status. What the heck was I supposed to do about that? I felt terrible just for existing. You dumped your white liberal guilt on me! Take it back!

- You said I looked like a pig! What kind of loving father would say that to a teenage daughter? You disowned any parts of your kids that didn't feed your ego. I've got news for you, we're not here for you to trot out when it impresses your friends or stay hidden when we might be an embarrassment. We have our own lives.

I didn't say these things directly to the person, just out loud in therapy or by myself. Some people do it directly. Before you make that choice, ask yourself, what is to be gained by doing this directly? Do I want to punish them or free myself?

Every time I stood up for myself, I felt stronger. I took back a piece of myself that was still hiding in fear and shame. I told the little girl she was safe now and it was okay to come out. I did *not* look for my part in it. I had no power as a child, therefore no responsibility. I've heard some sponsors say that our part in it was carrying it around for twenty years after it happened. I say BS to that! Was it supposed to magically disappear? We didn't know what to do.

We need to get angry about the abuse. Most of us want to brush it off, saying, oh, they didn't mean it, or they did a lot of good things, too, or they didn't know any better. All those things may be true. But look at *your* life. You are here in AA, admitting that your life isn't working. You have repressed feelings that need to come out. This exercise doesn't hurt them; they don't even know about it. You do this for yourself.

The end goal is forgiveness. We want to free ourselves from these resentments for our own sake. But it takes time and work. The only way out is through.

Resentments Affecting My Self-Esteem

I had many resentments against people who "made me feel bad about myself" (so I thought). I had not at some point stepped on their toes, bringing the situation upon myself, like the *Big Book* says. What actually happened was the person said something that triggered a reaction in me. I blamed them for doing that to me. They had "pushed one of my buttons." They were not responsible for my having that button. *It is my responsibility to get rid of the button, not punish the people who push it.* For example, once when we were first living together, my husband asked me, "How come you don't tap your toothbrush on the sink before putting it back in the stand?" I had never heard of that; I had never thought of that; I felt exposed and foolish. He "made me feel bad about myself." If I didn't have that big shame button, I could have said, "Oh, that's a good idea."

When I did my first Fourth Step, in the "How did it affect me?" column, it was always my self-esteem. That's my old way of thinking. But this is a complete mischaracterization of what self-esteem actually is—*how I feel about myself,* not how others see me. When I have boundaries, I can withstand someone's disapproval without changing how I feel about myself. When I'm seeking approval or validation from other people and don't get it, I mistake that as hurting my self-esteem. The problem is in me, seeking that approval or other-esteem in order to feel good about myself. The esteem of others is not the same thing as self-esteem. I do not have to change the way I feel about myself in reaction to what others say or do.

How Does It Affect Me?

Sometimes it's hard to get at the underlying misconception that creates an unwarranted or oversized fear or resentment. I freeze up at just having the feeling. The underlying, unconscious belief or fear is still unconscious. I know I'm upset with someone, but why? I find it helpful to force myself to complete the sentence: Because if this happens, it means (blank). *There's what's actually happening and then there's the story we tell ourselves about what's happening.* For example, someone doesn't call or text me back right away and I'm certain they have abandoned me, when in fact they haven't seen my message yet. Sometimes we've never verbalized the story and may not be conscious of it. The stories are frequently full of bad assumptions, misconceptions, and unexamined old ideas. One of mine was I cannot even entertain the thought that my marriage may be falling apart. Complete the sentence: If my marriage falls apart, it means…that I am a complete failure as a human being. Now take a step back. Do I know people who are divorced? Yes, lots of them. Do I think they are failures? No, not at all. Can I grant myself the same grace I grant them?

My thinking I shouldn't buy a house on a corner was the same thing—it means this realtor doesn't know what she's talking about! Oh, wait, let's examine the context in which I first had this idea and compare it to now. The side yards are different. Remember also that I had to ask her to explain. Old ideas are so familiar we accept them without question, but others can help us see things differently.

I've had a few bosses I just hated working for. It was demoralizing. They were people who I thought lacked the technical expertise to manage engineers. Why did it get under my skin every single day when it didn't seem to bother others that much? I don't know. Fill in the blank. Because if I have to report to an incompetent (in my opinion) person, it means (blank). It means he's valued more highly than I am, which means I'm worse than someone I see as incompetent. Wait a minute, we have different jobs. He's a manager, I'm an engineer. We're being evaluated by different standards. The manager doesn't have to be the best engineer (which isn't me anyway); that would be a waste of the best engineer.

Fears Inventory

The *Big Book* doesn't teach us how to process our fears. It says to admit that our reliance on self has failed and to turn to God to make them go away. I found it valuable to look at my fears and analyze them. It's sort of an exercise in risk management. This is how I can learn the skill of talking myself off the ledge. Let's work through some examples.

I'm afraid everyone thinks I'm fat. Is that a realistic fear? I know by now, through my own research, that this is of little to no interest for the vast majority of people and they are thinking about themselves, not me. Okay, so I'm projecting. But it's still constantly on my mind. Am I actually fat? By empirical standards (what size I wear, BMI, etc.), no. That's my distorted body image talking. This fear is fancied, not real. When it crops up, I remind myself of that.

I'm afraid of losing family relationships due to religious differences. Specifically, my grandchildren will be taught that I'm going to hell because I'm not of their faith. Is there anything I can do about it? Yes, I can be a consistently loving and supportive mother and grandmother and stay out of religious discussions with them. I can't predict the future, but it may not become a big issue unless *I* make it one. So, I won't do that. This is a speculative fear, and I have the power to mitigate the risk. I acknowledge that I have this fear, but I have a plan for dealing with it and will not dwell on it anymore.

I'm afraid of climate change. This is a real fear, but the burden of it is widely shared. I can only do so much. I will not engage in awfulizing—imagining horrific scenarios that may or may not happen. As a temporary fix for me personally, I can look into moving somewhere cooler if I decide it's worth it. I will also do my part to reduce human-caused climate change, but I will not do it perfectly or obsessively.

Harm to Self

In addition to the "Harm to Others" part of the inventory, it may benefit us to do a "Harm to Self" inventory. This is not to be an exercise in beating ourselves up. It has two purposes: to see how we might have handled the situation better (for future reference) and to see where we need to make living amends to ourselves. Make a list of situations that you came away from feeling really devalued, or like you didn't count, or you had been walked all over or taken advantage of, or when you compromised your values. For me, back when I was drinking, there were sexual situations I went along with when I didn't want to but didn't know how to get out of. There were lots of smaller situations, too—going along with something I didn't agree with or failing to defend myself because of my fear of confrontation—when I caved in and compromised myself.

Some situations may have very real fears or threats involved. I wouldn't stand up to a drunk, violent person who may actually injure me. I probably wouldn't tell off my boss if I wanted to keep my job. Sometimes, we have to walk away and deal with the feelings outside of people's presence. But often, the situation isn't that dire. Replay the scenario in your head and ask yourself, "What would a strong, self-confident person do in this situation?" They would stand up for themselves in some way or another. What prevented me from standing up for myself? Maybe some of these:

- Fear of confrontation
- Fear of their emotional reaction
- Fear they won't like me
- Fear of not fitting in
- Fear of abandonment
- The belief that it won't do any good
- The belief that I'm getting what I deserve
- The belief that if I challenge someone, I'm not being nice
- The belief that standing up for myself is putting my needs ahead of theirs, which is always wrong

We need to remind ourselves that these fears and beliefs came from our childhood and served a purpose back then, but they are holding us back today. Visualize your boundary in the situation. Where do you draw the line as to what is acceptable treatment of another human being and what you will not tolerate? How and when was this line crossed by the other person? Why did you let them cross it? Say out loud: "I have the right and the responsibility to define and defend my boundaries." What could you have done or said at that point to walk away from the situation with your head held high? Allowing people to invade our boundaries is not good for our sobriety or our self-esteem. Rehearse what you will do differently the next time a similar situation occurs. The more our self-esteem improves, the less we will find ourselves in these situations.

If this exercise brings you down on yourself, stop. You can do it another time, or not at all.

Here are some other ways we cause harm to ourselves:

- Smiling and saying yes when we want to say no
- Failing to acknowledge our achievements
- Blowing our mistakes all out of proportion
- Relentless self-criticism
- Reckless, dangerous, or self-destructive behavior
- Not allowing ourselves to have certain feelings
- Holding ourselves to impossibly high standards
- Not communicating our feelings, needs, and wants
- Tolerating another person's abusive behavior

If you think this list is helpful, continue to add your own examples. When you are done, look in the mirror and say something like this: "Hey, Bethie, I love you. I'm sorry you were not taught to value yourself. You treated yourself this way because you didn't know any different. You are lovable just the way you are, and you always have been. I will take care of you, be on your side, stand up for you, and learn all these new skills because you are worth it."

12

STEP FIVE

Admitted to God, to ourselves, and to another human being the exact nature of our wrongs.

Step Five is going over these lists with a trusted person, just like the *Big Book* says. I recommend not doing it with a dogmatic *Big Book* thumper, because they won't understand. They may say you are full of self-pity when you are simply feeling pain. They may say you are not taking responsibility when you were actually powerless. They may say to ask God to remove your fears and anger rather than processing them. (This is known as spiritual bypassing.) They may say harm to self is a selfish, self-centered exercise. But remember, Step Four was written for narcissists who did much harm to others. We mostly harmed ourselves, and it's just as important to see how and why we did that.

Shame is all about having secrets—we hide all the parts of ourselves we think make us unacceptable. We tend to think we're the only ones who feel the way we do and that we are alone because prior to AA there was no safe space to share and to listen to others like us. When we do Step Five with the right person, we will realize that many of the things we have felt so shameful about and hidden are actually fairly common in other people, too. We will begin to feel more like a part of the human race.

13

STEP SIX

Were entirely ready to have God remove all these defects of character.

I hate the word "defects." We probably have many of the same less-pre-ferred tendencies as most people, such as being impatient, intolerant, or judgmental. The *Big Book* covers these. But there are also undesirable behaviors that stem from having low self-esteem. The survival skills we developed in childhood to keep us safe sometimes go beyond that to mistreating other people. Here are a few of mine:

- I put other people down to feel better about myself.
- I disparage other people's accomplishments because they trigger my shame, as in, I should have done that.
- I have really high standards for myself in some areas (to ward off criticism), but then I judge or criticize others who don't live up to them.
- I categorically form negative opinions of groups that I think would reject me (I reject you first), without even giving them a chance.
- I question people's motives when they seem too nice or pay me a compliment.
- I lash out in anger when I feel threatened—"Well, you're not so perfect either!"

- I talk about people behind their backs because I don't have the courage to face them.
- I am passive-aggressive. I let people know when I'm upset without ever saying, "I'm upset with you."
- I try to get third parties involved in situations that only involve me and a different person because they can be used to carry messages or shore up my side two-against-one.
- I make it difficult for someone to tell me even one small criticism because they're afraid I will blow it all out of proportion.
- I find someone who is worse than me (like my husband with his drinking) and deflect the attention to their problems.

Most of these things don't rise to the level of harm to others that we put in Step Four. They're not like I stole from you, I slept with your significant other, I ruined your wedding, etc. But they are well worth our attention. Take some time while doing Step Six to note the ways your low self-esteem has manifested in behavior patterns like these. As we build our self-esteem, they will become unnecessary, but they still may be habitual. Changing habits takes work.

Less-preferred behaviors like these become habits because they work, on some level. They protect me, help me avoid confrontation, make me feel not as bad about myself, etc. As we contemplate giving them up, we will need to replace them with healthier behaviors. As we become more loving and accepting of ourselves (are you still doing the affirmations?), the need for them goes away.

14

STEP SEVEN

Humbly asked Him to remove our shortcomings.

When I was a newcomer, I read this step and thought, Well, if I do that, there'll be nothing left of me at all. My whole being is defective. It turns out, my single biggest "defect" (I hate that word) was my belief that I am defective. A host of other problems issued from that. I used to picture myself coming off the assembly line of little girls being made, not passing inspection, and being issued to an unfortunate family as a marked-down factory second. When I got sober, I was informed there was nothing inherently wrong with me—I had only been taught there was. Having this new knowledge changed nothing. I still had crippling shame for a long time in sobriety. During that time, I pictured an assembly line of little girls all alike, and the last step was to plug a chip into them that animated them with the belief that they were nice, normal girls. But they plugged a chip into me that said, "You're fat, dumb, ugly, and worthless." I may have looked like the others, but my programming made me different. It was almost as bad living with that knowledge as before.

Recovery takes a long time to work its way from the head to the heart.

For many years in recovery, I knew intellectually that the belief that I am defective was false, but, oh boy, did it have a lot of baggage attached to it that didn't go away automatically just because of new knowledge. *Insight does not equal behavioral change.* I can't become a good swimmer or golfer by reading books about it. I have to do the action to develop the skill. Today, I have been reprogrammed by AA and all the work I have done so that in my head and in my heart, I know I'm an okay person.

Because I grew up in a crazy-making environment, I acquired character traits that were specialized to work in that setting. I wasn't bad or defective. I don't want to have part of me excised or removed. I prefer a more holistic approach to Step Seven. I gather all these little soldiers, my defenders, around me and thank them for the job they did keeping me safe when I needed them. I love all of you, but your work is done. I'm an adult now, and I can take care of myself. I'm taking charge of my life, and you'll always be a part of it, but you are not in charge anymore. I have a loving and supportive community of recovering people around me now, and/or a Higher Power, and we will be taking it from here.

Of course, we don't expect our old habits to go away instantaneously. Remember the switching dominant hands example. We will likely not even notice the many times we resort to our old ways. With practice, we may see it after we do it. Later, we will catch ourselves while we're doing it and change course. Eventually, we will have new habits. We will lose them if we stop doing the self-reflection, stop attending meetings, or become complacent. Recovery is a lifelong journey.

15

STEP EIGHT

Made a list of all persons we had harmed, and became willing to make amends to them all.

Of course we will make amends to people we have harmed, just like it says in the *Big Book*. For some of us, acknowledging that we harmed others can stir up so much despair and remorse that we want to drink or destroy ourselves or spend days ruminating about how bad we are. None of this is helpful. If we agree we were in the grip of a progressive illness, or raised by wolves, we can acknowledge we were not able to be our best selves at the time or even see how we were causing harm. We can show ourselves the same compassion we would show to any other alcoholic in this situation. But, from the other person's perspective, we harmed them and we owe them amends.

I allowed a sober friend of mine to house-sit for me for two weeks because she needed a place to stay, and she started drinking right after I left. She caused harm. AA people had to get her out of my house; they took her to someone else's house, she refused to leave, and the police had to be called. My son came over and cleaned up the mess she left. Another friend had to come every day to take care of my pets. There were morning and evening chores, so some just didn't get done. No pets died, but I lost three houseplants. And I was stressed out thousands of miles away trying to take care of this during my vacation.

Several people were put out by her behavior. I could give her a list of people she owes amends to (but she hasn't asked). On the other hand, I also feel compassion for her because she is a sick alcoholic. I am still kind to her. And perhaps I had bad judgment in trusting her. Try to separate the specific harm you caused from who you are overall, in the big picture. Make amends for the specific harms. But have compassion for yourself rather than wallowing in remorse. *The harms we have caused don't define us. Just because I did something wrong doesn't mean there is something wrong with me. Just because I made a mistake, it doesn't mean I am a mistake.* One of the gifts of AA is that we hear people we love and respect tell about terrible things they did. We learn that we are lovable and respectable despite our past actions.

When we did Step Four, we also made a list of ways we had harmed ourselves. We must become willing to make those amends, too.

We often repeat behaviors that on the surface seem counterproductive because they have some kind of hidden payoff. We don't keep getting burned on a stove like we do in our interactions with others—if the consequences are all bad, we stop. Let's look at some of them.

I want to stop holding myself to impossibly high standards. It usually results in my feeling not good enough, causes a lot of stress, and turns me back into a martyr. What could I possibly be getting out of it that makes me keep doing it? On some level, I think it protects me from criticism. It makes everything look good on the outside so no one will look further. What might happen if I stop doing it? Someone might find fault with me. My whole house of cards will come crashing down. Can I let go of these fears, make a mistake in front of someone, and see that it's really no big deal? Do I want to have a house of cards or a strong foundation? Can I shift my focus onto who I am rather than how I look to others? I had a sponsee who signed up to chair a Zoom meeting several months down the road. She was consumed with learning to Zoom perfectly three months in advance. I told her that while I respected her willingness to learn the technology, it would probably provide more growth for her to do it imperfectly and see that no one cares, rather than learn how to do it perfectly.

I want to stop prejudging people, inventing a story about something being wrong with them. What is the payoff when I do that? In my mind, I'm sure they're going to reject me, so I protect myself by not giving them the chance. Can I start to give people a chance and find that my fears of rejection are largely unfounded? I had been talking to a woman in a class for several weeks and we enjoyed our conversations. One day, she mentioned she had been a dancer for a professional basketball team. And I must have mentioned I was a lawyer. I told her, "You know I probably wouldn't have talked to you if I had known you were a dancer, because I'd think that you think you're better than me." She said, "I probably wouldn't have talked to you if I had known you were a lawyer, because I'd think I wasn't smart enough." We both laughed.

These are just a couple examples of becoming ready to make amends to ourselves. We look these self-harming behaviors over and for the most part see that while they may have protected us at one time, now they are more of a hindrance. We become willing to try new behaviors that may bring more joy into our lives.

16

STEP NINE

Made direct amends to such people wherever possible, except when to do so would injure them or others.

The *Big Book* has plenty to offer on how to make amends to others. Most of the harm caused by egomaniacs is harm to others. Although we have harmed others (who in this world hasn't?) and will make those amends, we have likely caused ourselves the most harm.

Remember that we started out as precious little innocent children. We had a spark of life; we were full of potential; the world was ours to explore. Somewhere along the line, that was taken from us. I always blamed myself. Then I started drinking. "Like a river that don't know where it's flowin', I took a wrong turn and I just kept goin."[50]

One of the best experiences we can ever have in AA is seeing a twinkle return to the eyes of a newcomer. That's what we want for ourselves, too, and we deserve it.

We have a list of the ways we harmed ourselves from Step Four, and we also took an honest look at why we might hang on to some of these behaviors. We saw that many of them were survival skills we learned when we were "fighting in Iraq," but they were double-edged swords that protected us but also hurt us. We are not in Iraq anymore. We don't need them. What a relief that is!

Let's take, for example, failure to acknowledge our achievements. Make a list of your past accomplishments—graduations, jobs, promotions, performances, contests, things that were hard but you got through them, losing weight, quitting smoking, getting in shape, finishing a big project, staying sober for however long it's been—anything you feel the slightest bit proud of. Spend some time with each one. Savor it. Say, "Yes, that was me! I did that! Way to go, me! I'm proud of myself." One of the biggest amends I made to myself was going back to school, going from being a college-dropout to person with three degrees.

What can we do about blowing our mistakes all out of proportion? Revisit the situation. I was part of it, and it turned out badly. What other factors were involved? My friend was an elementary school teacher, and her students weren't testing well in math. Being one of us, she naturally concluded it was because she was a bad teacher. I started asking her, "Did you choose the curriculum? Did you decide the best way for your kids to learn was to make them sit at desks all day? Are the kids coming from homes where there's dysfunction or poverty? Do you know what they had for breakfast on the day of the test? Did they get enough sleep?" She finally could see that she may be one part of the system but she doesn't control the system.

Or suppose I chair an online meeting and don't know how to use the technology like a pro. Am I mortified by my stupidity, irresponsibility, lack of respect for others in the meeting who are counting on me? I could tell myself these things, but before I am even done, someone else will say, "I got it," and the meeting will go on. These people do not expect me to be perfect and are just glad someone stepped up to chair the meeting. If one of them didn't know how to do something, would I think they were stupid, irresponsible, and disrespectful? Not at all. I grant myself the same leeway I grant others.

Many of our amends will be living amends. We are learning how to treat ourselves better. We will allow ourselves a few "indulgences" once in a while. We will take better care of our health. We will replace our critical voice with affirmations. We will not do any more dangerous, reckless behaviors that show little regard for our health, lives, and others. We will not poison ourselves with alcohol and drugs. We will remind ourselves that we are human; therefore, we will make mistakes and not do things perfectly, and that's perfectly fine. My new standard for housecleaning isn't spotless, it's substantial improvement. If it's worth doing, it's worth doing poorly. We will learn who we are and be true to ourselves. We will communicate our needs and desires and not expect or hope that others can read our minds. We will be honest with ourselves and others. We will live by our own values and standards and stop worrying about what others may think. We were making all that up, anyway. We will treat ourselves the way we treat something that is precious, unique, special, and valuable because that's what we are.

17

STEP TEN

Continued to take personal inventory, and when we were wrong promptly admitted it.

When we do Step Ten, let's first look at what we did right today. We are not in the habit of acknowledging our successes.

- Did I stay sober?
- Did I try something new today?
- Did I use an AA tool to help me with a situation?
- Did I accept a compliment?
- Did I notice something pleasant?
- Did I do something kind, not motivated by codependency?
- Was I gentle with myself, not demanding perfection?
- Did I worry about what other people might think a little less than I used to?
- Did I allow myself to have a feeling and handle it appropriately?
- Did I make progress with any goal, even though I'm not there yet?
- Did I reach out to another alcoholic?

This is not a complete checklist. It's some ideas to get you started. Try to come up with at least ten things every day. For each thing you put on your list, pause a moment and give yourself credit. *Recovery can feel overwhelming if we don't take time out to notice our improvements on the way.* If it was an awful day but you stayed sober, give yourself a big hand for that.

Once you've completed this list, you may start to feel selfish (because you just spent time focusing on yourself or tooting your own horn). If so, make another list of ten things you did today that benefitted others. It can be as mundane as cooking, cleaning, working to support your family, emptying the trash, chatting with a neighbor, giving a ride, calling a friend. You probably do many things every day for others you don't give yourself credit for.

Now we can look at some things that maybe didn't go so well, without losing sight of the big picture, which is that *we are doing a courageous job changing our lives and we are making progress.*

When I look at who I may have harmed that day and may need to make amends to, I include myself. Remember, unlike Bill being on a power drive and stepping on people's toes, we have mostly harmed ourselves. Did I sell myself out or sell myself short? Did I say yes when my gut was screaming no? Did I pick up a drink? Okay, so I fell short today. Good time to practice self-compassion. "Hey, Bethie, I'm sorry I let you down today. I'm new at this and it's hard. I love you, and I will try to do better tomorrow."

As far as others go, I take this step a little deeper than the *Big Book*. It's more than *I was wrong, I apologize* (although that's a good start). If we really want to have a personality change sufficient to overcome alcoholism, we have to look at our motivations and unconscious drives. We need to become conscious of them to change them. The big question in Step Ten for me is "What drove me to do (or say) that?"

This endeavor took me straight into looking at defense mechanisms. Defense mechanisms are meant to protect us from things that are difficult to face.[51] We acquired many of them in childhood as responses to the environments we were living in. Narcissism itself is basically one big defense mechanism: I'm going to be the best to protect myself from feeling like the worst. Placating, appeasing, and codependency are defense mechanisms that also become character traits. On a daily basis, people deny, minimize, rationalize, justify, intellectualize, and project.[52] By learning to identify defense mechanisms, I began to see when I was employing them.

Projection is an interesting one—instead of admitting that we judge ourselves, we say, "People will think…" We think the judgment is coming from outside us when it's really coming from us.[53] Here's how I work on my projecting: I made this choice because otherwise everyone would think…stop right there. Everyone? Well if it's that widespread, name three people you know with absolute certainty would think that. If you get that far, now go and ask them what they actually think. I usually asked other people in AA because they could understand what I was doing. Now I know it's me doing the judging. So, where did I get this standard I think I have to live up to? Do I even agree with it? Holding myself to incredibly high standards was fear-based—this is the standard by which no one can find fault with me. We have no insight into or control over what others are thinking. Most of the time they are thinking about their own lives. People who want to find fault will find fault. I need to focus on setting my own standards that I'm comfortable with.

When I do Step Ten and realize I reacted out of defensiveness, the deeper look is, why did I become defensive? In what way did I feel threatened? Because I couldn't let what happen? Because if that happened it would mean (blank). Sometimes it was social status. I was afraid of looking bad in public. I used the esteem of others as a substitute for self-esteem, so I couldn't afford to have others think badly of me. Other times the fear was of being unmasked—someone might see through my act and discover my defectiveness. Today, I am more secure inside myself and don't worry as much about what others think. I work hard at being authentic rather than trying to convince people I'm something I'm not.

Was there some truth that I found unpalatable? Instead of denying or minimizing, I try to understand why I was fighting it. Some part of me feels threatened by it. Because if that were true, it would mean (blank). I examine the truthfulness of the story I'm telling myself. It may be outdated or never true to begin with. Bill's story comes to mind—if he wasn't the best, it meant he was the worst.

Step Ten in the *Twelve & Twelve* has some really good stuff about looking at our motives. It's easy to hide a bad motive under a good one. Sometimes I took care of things my husband was supposed to do (what a loving gesture!), secretly hoping it would make him feel guilty. Sponsors can help us identify our hidden agendas. We need help to see our blind spots. As we gain more insight into our behavior, we will gradually become more capable of rigorous honesty and not be able to fool ourselves about our underlying intent.

We codependents have to look at our motives when we are people-pleasing, giving, volunteering, and caretaking. We may find our motive is to feel better about ourselves; to avoid confrontation; to get people to like us; or because when we say no, we feel guilty. These are the old behaviors we are trying to change. While the program encourages service work and being there for others, we need to have something inside of us to give, first. We have to give it away to keep it, but first, we have to *get* it. The best giving comes from a full and grateful heart, not an empty one. As long as our motives are honest and true to ourselves, we can give all we want.

18

STEP ELEVEN

Sought through prayer and meditation to improve our conscious contact with God as we understood Him, asking only for knowledge of His will for us and the power to carry that out.

The Serenity Prayer is a great prayer. I'd like to point out that in the prayer, we ask for serenity first, which gives us some distance from what's going on so that we can reflect on acceptance and courage and choose our path. For me, "serenity" generally means a change in perception or perspective. Sometimes it's as simple as zooming in or zooming out of the situation. I'm hung up on something small and can't see the big picture. Or I'm overwhelmed by something huge and can't see that my feet are still on the ground and the sun still comes up every day. I need a new way of seeing the situation before I can accept it. Remember, it's a process.

The reason I mention it is because in the story *Doctor, Alcoholic, Addict*[54] (now called *Acceptance Was the Answer*), Dr. Paul states that he can have no serenity until he accepts. He gets it backward. I have tried to follow his guidance, attempting to bludgeon myself into acceptance of something, and it has never worked. I recommend doing the whole feelings process, acknowledging I don't like this, I wish it wasn't this way, I'm angry and I feel trapped—venting the emotional energy instead of trying to stuff it by demanding acceptance right from the get-go. Then I can use other tools to change my perspective. The easiest one is to ask other people their perspective. Or, I can see if I'm telling myself a story about it that isn't really true. Or, it may be true but there's nothing I can do about it, and having exhausted all other options, I will gradually fall into acceptance.

Meditation can be used to enhance our self-esteem. Meditation actually helps rewire the brain.[55] Instead of identifying with the hamster wheel going around in our heads, we can just watch it. When thoughts and feelings pop up during meditation, we can just let them go; we don't have to run with them; we can just observe them. *We will begin to see who we are as separate from what goes on in our heads.* The true self is a calm space. Meditation is also very helpful for people who have a highly reactive nervous system. If you are unable to pause when agitated or doubtful because the reaction happened so fast you lost the ability to stop and think, meditation can help train your nervous system to be less reactive.

The *Big Book* talks a lot about self-monitoring in this section. It says to check in with God many times each day and ask for the next right thought or action. That's fine, but it's also necessary to check in with ourselves several times a day. It may be the same thing. *God, am I doing what you want me to be doing?* also involves self-reflection. I had the old habit of monitoring other people's moods, feelings, and needs so that I could feel safe. It's more important to recognize what kind of mood I am in, what I am feeling, whether I have any unmet needs that I can take care of or seek help for. If I am in a bad mood, I need to acknowledge it and not take it out on those around me. A parent can be in a bad mood and let the child know it's not about them instead of letting it fall on them. That's modeling how to handle a bad mood, a good example for a child. This is another aspect of owning our feelings—it's better for the people around us, too.

If I am angry and recognize it, I need to go through the process previously described to vent and then choose my response instead of having a knee-jerk reaction.

I am apparently still wired to avoid confrontation, and I tend to find out I'm angry after the fact when I spend the next couple hours replaying the scene in my head and inventing snappy comebacks. One time, I was driving on the freeway with another woman in the program and she asked me if I'd mind putting more space between me and the car in front of me. My foot was on the brake before she finished the sentence, even though the amount of space looked fine to me.

The next day I woke up fuming: "I've been driving since I was sixteen years old! I commute downtown during rush hour every single day! You don't even own a car!" I was in the venting process a day late. Since anger is a response to a perceived threat, I ask myself in what way did I feel threatened. She said I was a bad driver. Why does that bother me? Because I think I'm a good driver, but now I don't know who to trust and I feel insecure. In an area where I once had self-confidence, I was now experiencing self-doubt. After venting, here's my conclusion: It doesn't matter what she thinks. Self-esteem comes from within, not from the approval of others. I don't have to give her the power to determine how I feel about myself. And from now on, it couldn't hurt to pay closer attention to how much space there is between me and the other cars on the highway.

If my feelings are hurt and I'm feeling small or less than, I need to do some affirmations or talk to a friend and build myself back up again. I remind myself that I am okay with or without this person's approval, even if I made a mistake or did something embarrassing. I may need to shore up my boundaries and realize that it's more about the other person than it is about me. I remind myself there's always more than one possible explanation for someone's behavior. Don't overinterpret; don't take it personally. Maybe they're just having a bad day.

AA people always say not to let someone "rent space in your head," but I never received any instruction on how to do that. So naturally, when it happened, I thought I was doing recovery wrong, another failure. Turns out it's another one of those things that's a process; I can't command it out of my head. I have to do the slow walk through—feel the feeling, express it, ask why does this bother me so much, etc., like I did with the driving example.

19

STEP TWELVE

Having had a spiritual experience as the result of these steps, we tried to carry this message to alcoholics and practice these principles in all our affairs.[56]

Bill's spiritual awakening was the acknowledgment that he was not God, that he was not in charge, that being a "worker among workers" in the end created a more satisfying and fulfilling life than the power-driven Bill could ever have achieved.

We, on the other hand, have been striving not so much for power but for a feeling of security, which we lacked internally but thought we could find by achieving, getting the approval of others, the right relationship, alcohol—anything that could fleetingly suggest to us that maybe we were okay. Because we had learned to hide our true natures, we, too, were lacking that feeling of connection that Bill and Bob felt when they first sat down and talked. The best thing about AA, to me, is that you can say I don't feel very good about myself and someone else will say me too. Because it's safe to be vulnerable, we begin to learn how to connect. We begin to see ourselves and others as more alike than different.

In the *Spiritual Experience*,[57] it says we have tapped an unsuspected inner resource, which they call God. For me, I *developed* an unsuspected resource. It was me! It was there all along, but way under-developed. I grew it with your help by being a part of the AA community; becoming honest, vulnerable, and authentic; working the Steps; having a sponsor; and being loved all along the way. I don't feel so rudderless in a storm anymore. The feeling of having a secure home base I didn't have in childhood is now in me but relies on my maintaining connection with you.

The story doesn't end there. Before, we were trying to flex our "helpful" muscles in service of others, but we lacked core strength. All these exercises have developed our inner strength so that we can have a solid base from which we reach out. Self-esteem isn't the holy grail, just like core strength isn't the end goal of weightlifting. But we are much more effective when we have it. Working with newcomers who are like I used to be remains a big part of my life today. So many have never had a solid, sober adult in their life who loves them just the way they are. I'm able to be that for my sponsees and give people hope when I share in meetings. People out there are suffering and dying because they've never been told they deserve better. They don't know they're lovable. It hurts my heart for anyone to feel that way. We used to be them. Now we can help them.

ENDNOTES

1   Bill Wilson et al., Big Book of Alcoholics Anonymous. New York: AA World Services, 2001, originally published in 1939.

2   Alcoholics Anonymous, Twelve Steps and Twelve Traditions. New York: AA World Services, 2009, originally published in 1952.

3   *Big Book*, chapter five.

4   Nor were there actually one hundred men. He told an interviewer in 1954 that he said a hundred to make it sound good, like it was really going to work. Schaberg, William (2019). Writing the Big Book: The Creation of A.A. NV: Central Recovery Press, unnumbered page before Table of Contents.

5   Alcoholics Anonymous Comes of Age (AACOA), AA World Services, 1989.

6   An ACE score is a tally of different types of abuse, neglect, and other hallmarks of a rough childhood. According to the Adverse Childhood Experiences study, the rougher your childhood, the higher your score is likely to be and the higher your risk for later health problems. https://americanspcc.org/take-the-aces-quiz/ visited July 1, 2020.

7   Co-dependency, https://www.mhanational.org/conditions/co-dependency (n.d.) Retrieved August 3, 2020.

8   Ibid.

9   Codependents Anonymous, https://coda.org/wp-content/uploads/2020/07/Am-I-Co-Dependent-Bro-4002.pdf. Retrieved January 11, 2021.

10   https://dictionary.cambridge.org/us/dictionary/english/ego

11   https://www.merriam-webster.com/dictionary/self

12   AACOA. AA World Services, 1989.

13   Hesse, Monica, 2020. "The Weird Masculinity of Donald Trump." Washington Post. https://www.washingtonpost.com/lifestyle/style/the-weird-masculinity-of-donald-trump/2020/07/15/0dfe3854-c43e-11ea-b037-f9711f89ee46 story.html

14   AACOA. AA World Services, 1989.

15   Tiebout, Dr. Harry (1944). "Therapeutic Mechanism of Alcoholics Anonymous." The American Journal of Psychiatry, January, 1944. (Also reprinted in Appendix E of AACOA.)

16   Ibid.

17   I wish I had read Dr. Tiebout's article thirty-five years ago and realized that the whole Higher Power thing is only in there for narcissists. It was a complete red herring as far as my problems went. It would have saved me a lot of heart-

ache over not fitting in.

18 Malkin, Craig (2015). Rethinking Narcissism: The Secret to Recognizing and Coping with Narcissists. New York: HarperCollins.

19 Malkin, C. (2017). The Narcissism Test. Retrieved from https://www.drcraig-malkin.com/#narcissismtest.

20 https://www.mayoclinic.org/diseases-conditions/narcissistic-personality-disorder/symptoms-causes/syc-20366662 visited July 1, 2020.

21 Kaufman, Gershen (1989). The Psychology of Shame: Theory and Treatment of Shame-Based Syndromes. New York: Springer Publishing Co.

22 Engel, Beverly (2006). Healing Your Emotional Self. Hoboken, NJ: John Wiley & Sons.

23 Brown, Brené (2010). The Gifts of Imperfection. Center City, MN: Hazelden.

24 Tolstoy, Leo (1878). Anna Karenina.

25 I'm afraid people will read my story, see that my mother was a one-of-a-kind wacko, and use that to distance themselves from my message. I hope that's not the case. None of us want to think badly of our families, but look at the results they've produced.

26 https://www.cdc.gov/violenceprevention/aces/about.html

27 https://www.cdc.gov/violenceprevention/pdf/essentials-for-childhood-framework508.pdf.

28 An ongoing area of study is trans-generational trauma being passed down via epigenetics. Maybe some of us are born at a disadvantage. Who knows? It may invalidate this entire book. Either that or gut bacteria. The trick is to find something that makes sense to us, given what we know now.

29 Cori, Jasmin (2010). The Emotionally Absent Mother: A Guide to Self-healing and Getting the Love You Missed. New York: The Experiment, LLC.

30 National Scientific Council on the Developing Child (2004.) "Children's Emotional Development Is Built into the Architecture of their Brains: Working Paper No. 2." Harvard Center for the Developing Child. Retrieved from https://developingchild.harvard.edu/resources/childrens-emotional-development-is-built-into-the-architecture-of-their-brains/.

31 Eagleman, David (2015). The Brain: The Story of You, A Companion to the PBS Series. New York: Pantheon Books.

32 https://www.cdc.gov/violenceprevention/aces/about.html

33 Golomb, Elan (1992). Trapped in the Mirror: Adult Children of Narcissists in Their Struggle for Self. New York: William Morrow.

34 Walker, Pete (2014). Complex PTSD: From Surviving to Thriving. Coppell, TX: Azure Coyote.

35 See, e.g., "Big Impact of Microaggressions" (Gehrman 2020); "How Racism

and Microaggressions Lead to Worse Health" (Torini 2017).

36 Yoon, Hahna (2020). "How to Respond to Microaggressions." New York Times, March 3, 2020.

37 There's no one right way to parent or be parented. During our evolutionary history, when most children didn't live to be five years old, not nearly as many resources were put into their development. In some cultures they weren't even named till they turned five. In many societies, the purpose of having kids has been to put them to work as soon as possible and take care of their parents in old age.

Today's goal in our society—"be all you can be"—is a very Western, egocentric model of the self. Most non-Western cultures have a different conception of the self that is sociocentric rather than egocentric. In an anthropology class, we reviewed a test given to people from different cultures, who were asked to finish ten sentences that began with the words "I am." Subjects in Western cultures listed individual traits: I'm tall, I'm an engineer, I'm successful, etc. Non-Western subjects tended to give answers more along the lines of: I'm a (name of clan, family group, surname—whatever locates them in a kinship community), I'm x's mother, I'm y's wife, z's employee, etc. A man from South Korea in the class flat out said, "We would never start ten sentences in a row with 'I.'"

In Western educated industrialized rich democracies (WEIRD cultures), we have very few children and pump tons of resources into them. It takes a long time before there's any return on the investment. We are generally trying to produce adults who are happy, productive members of society who live up to their potential. I am writing within the WEIRD paradigm that is by no means universal.

There is also no such thing as a perfect parent, and it is not required. "Good enough" is the standard. Letting children know you are fallible gives them permission to be fallible, too.

38 McLeod, Saul (2020). Maslow's Hierarchy of Needs. Retrieved from https://www.simplypsychology.org/maslow.html.

39 The highest on his list is self-actualization, and several people have also recommended transcendence (moving beyond the self) to be added along with it. These would be our goals as adults, working Step Twelve. Many of us have been helping others without having had the basic needs met first, which is why our helping derails into codependency.

40 I heard him say this on a Zoom seminar called "Addiction and Trauma," put on by The Meadows Behavioral Health and PESI, Inc., October 16, 2020.

41 Larsen & Hegarty (1987). Days of Healing, Days of Joy: Daily Meditations for Adult Children. New York: Harper & Row.

42 Ibid.

43 Goleman, D. (1995). Emotional Intelligence. New York: Bantam.

44 Heflick, N. (2011, November 23). "The Spotlight Effect." Retrieved from Psychology Today: https://www.psychologytoday.com/us/blog/the-big-questions/201111/the-spotlight-effect.

45 It was a proud moment for me when I witnessed this: I was riding in the car with my son, and his four-year-old son was in the back seat. The child complained about being stuck in traffic because the scenery wasn't changing. My son didn't tell him to quit his whining. He said, "You know what, kiddo? I don't like it either. We can't do anything about the traffic. Let's make up a game to pass the time." Serenity Prayer in action!

46 Gladwell, Malcolm (2008). Outliers: The Story of Success. NY: Little, Brown, & Co.

47 Engel, Beverly (2006). Healing Your Emotional Self. Hoboken, NJ: John Wiley & Sons; Earley & Weiss (2013). Freedom from Your Inner Critic. Boulder: Sounds True, Inc; Walker, Pete (2014). Complex PTSD: From Surviving to Thriving. Coppell, TX: Azure Coyote.

48 The Twelve Steps are taken from the first edition of the *Big Book* (Wilson, 1939), which is no longer under copyright.

49 I forced myself to get over this fear by throwing a couple baby showers for women in the program. People came over, but I didn't feel like I was the center of attention, so it was easier. Baby steps.

50 "Everybody's Got a Hungry Heart," Bruce Springsteen.

51 Burgo, Joseph (2012). Why Do I Do That? Psychological Defense Mechanisms and the Hidden Ways They Shape Our Lives. Chapel Hill: New Rise Press.

52 That little alcoholic voice in my head (the evil genius) uses all these tricks, too, to talk me into drinking again. You're not really an alcoholic (denial); it wasn't that bad (minimize); you deserve it after a day like this (justify); people think you're weird because you don't drink (projection); etc. That parasite feels threatened and is fighting to stay alive.

53 A more severe type of projection is the kind my mother did: I deny anything being wrong with me. It's all you.

54 Dr. Paul O's story in the *Big Book*.

55 Hanson, Rick (2009). Buddha's Brain: The Practical Neuroscience of Happiness, Wisdom, and Love. Oakland: New Harbinger Publications.

56 "Spiritual experience" was changed to "spiritual awakening" in later editions of the *Big Book*.

57 Appendix II in the *Big Book*.

BIBLIOGRAPHY

AA World Services. (1989) (14th printing). *AA Comes of Age*. New York: AA World Services.

Beatty, M. (1986). *Codependent No More*. Center City, MN: Hazelden.

Brown, B. (2010). *The Gifts of Imperfection*. Center City, MN: Hazelden.

Burgo, J. (2012). *Why Do I Do That? Psychological Defense Mechanisms and the Hidden Ways They Shape Our Lives*. Chapel Hill: New Rise Press.

Codependents Anonymous. (2015). *Am I Codependent?* Retrieved from Codependents Anonymous: https://coda.org/wp-content/uploads/2020/07/Am-I-Co-Dependent-Bro-4002.pdf.

Cori, J. (2010). *The Emotionally Absent Mother: A Guide to Self-healing and Getting the Love You Missed*. New York: The Experiment, LLC.

Eagleman, D. (2015). *The Brain: The Story of You, A Companion to the PBS Series*. New York: Pantheon Books.

Earley, J., & Weiss, B. (2013). *Freedom from Your Inner Critic*. Boulder: Sounds True, Inc.

Engel, B. (2006). *Healing Your Emotional Self*. Hoboken, NJ: John Wiley & Sons.

Friel, J., & Friel, L. (2010). *Adult Children: The Secrets of Dysfunctional Families*. Deerfield Beach, FL: Health Communications, Inc.

Gibson, L. (2015). *Adult Children of Emotionally Immature Parents: How to Heal from Distant, Rejecting, or Self-Involved Parents.* Oakland, CA: New Harbinger Publications.

Goleman, D. (1995). *Emotional Intelligence.* New York: Bantam.

Golomb, E. (1992). *Trapped in the Mirror: Adult Children of Narcissists in Their Struggle for Self.* New York: William Morrow.

Hanson, R. (2009). *Buddha's Brain: The Practical Neuroscience of Happiness, Love, and Wisdom.* Oakland, CA: New Harbinger Publications.

Heflick, N. (2011, November 23). *"The Spotlight Effect."* Retrieved from *Psychology Today*: https://www.psychologytoday.com/us/blog/the-big-questions/201111/the-spotlight-effect.

Hesse, M. (2020, July 16). "The Weird Masculinity of Donald Trump." *Washington Post.* Retrieved from https://www.washington-post.com/lifestyle/style/the-weird-masculinity-of-donald-trump/2020/07/15/0dfe3854-c43e-11ea-b037-f9711f89ee46_story.html.

Kaufman, G. (1989). *The Psychology of Shame: Theory and Treatment of Shame-Based Syndromes.* New York: Springer Publishing Co.

Larsen, E., & Hegarty, C. (1987). *Days of Healing Days of Joy: Daily Meditations for Adult Children.* New York: Harper & Row.

Malkin, C. (2015). *Rethinking Narcissism: The Secret to Recognizing and Coping with Narcissists.* New York: HarperCollins.

Malkin, C. (2017). *The Narcissism Test.* Retrieved from Dr. Craig Malkin: https://www.drcraigmalkin.com/#narcissismtest.

Mayo Clinic. (2020, May 21). "*Narcissistic Personality Disorder.*" Retrieved from Mayo Clinic: https://www.mayoclinic.org/diseases-conditions/narcissistic-personality-disorder/symptoms-causes/syc-20366662.

McLeod, S. (2020, March 20). *Maslow's Hierarchy of Needs.* Retrieved from *Simple Psychology*: https://www.simplypsychology.org/maslow.html.

Mellody, P. (1989). *Facing Codependence.* San Francisco: Harper.

National Scientific Council on the Developing Child. (2004). "*Children's Emotional Development Is Built into the Architecture of their Brains: Working Paper No. 2.*" Retrieved from Harvard Center for the Developing Child: https://developingchild.harvard.edu/resources/childrens-emotional-development-is-built-into-the-architecture-of-their-brains/.

Tiebout, H. (1944, January). "Therapeutic Mechanism of Alcoholics Anonymous." *The American Journal of Psychiatry*, 468-473.

Tolstoy, L. (1878). *Anna Karenina.*

Walker, P. (2014). *Complex PTSD: From Surviving to Thriving.* Contra Costa, CA: Azure Coyote Publishing.

Wilson, B. (1961, April). "God As We Understand Him: The Dilemma of No Faith." *The Grapevine.*

Wilson, B. (2001). *Alcoholics Anonymous.* New York: A.A. World Services, Inc.

Wilson, B. (2009). *Twelve Steps and Twelve Traditions.* New York: A.A. World Services, Inc.

Yoon, H. (2020, March 3). "How to Respond to Microaggressions." *New York Times*. Retrieved March 3, 2020, from https://www.nytimes.com/2020/03/03/smarter-living/how-to-respond-to-microaggressions.html?searchResultPosition=1.